Torsten Husén
Conversations in Comparative Education

by
Arild Tjeldvoll

edited by
Hans G. Lingens

Phi Delta Kappa Educational Foundation
Bloomington, Indiana U.S.A.

Cover design by
Victoria Voelker

Photographic assistance by
Vladimir Bektesh

Photographs throughout this book are from Torsten Husén's
personal collection and are used with his permission.

Phi Delta Kappa Educational Foundation
408 North Union Street
Post Office Box 789
Bloomington, Indiana 47402-0789
U.S.A.

Printed in the United States of America

Library of Congress Catalog Card Number 00-101819
ISBN 0-87367-824-9
Copyright © 2000 by Phi Delta Kappa Educational Foundation

*This book is sponsored by the
Sweden Tercentenary Bank Foundation,
which made a generous contribution
toward publication costs.*

Table of Contents

Editor's Preface

For international and comparative educators all over the world, Torsten Husén needs no introduction. Husén has been at the forefront of the development of this discipline, and these pages show what an important role he has played at all levels and in all the facets of international and comparative education. He is one of the few great educators who has a gestalt of national and global education. He sees the necessity to learn other languages and to emerge from provincial thinking and planning in order to seek examples and experiences in other countries to deal with issues at home.

Through his cross-national studies and experiences, Husén learned to look at education using a multifaceted historical and cultural perspective as a necessary condition for change. Not only does he explain how international and comparative education came together in the beginning, but he also describes the role and the reason for the inception of many education agencies, both national and international in scope.

From this biography, drawn from his conversations with Arild Tjeldvoll, readers will learn that Husén truly is a world educator deeply grounded in practice and theory. Torsten Husén has much to tell us about the paths that education in the Western countries is taking and the choices that underdeveloped nations are making. There is much to ponder here for future studies in this area.

Arild Tjeldvoll, also a respected comparative educator, has captured the essence of Husén through conversation. His thorough knowledge of the discipline has allowed him to ask pertinent questions and to capture Torsten Husén's thoughts in a highly accessible manner. It has been a pleasure to work with this material, knowing that this book will make available to all the essence of a great and humble thinker and researcher in international and comparative education.

Hans G. Lingens

Introduction and Acknowledgments

On the front page of *Prospect's Quarterly Review of Education* (Vol. 23, no. 3/4, 1993, pp. 87-88) the journal's editors listed 25 "thinkers on education," historically and worldwide. Three were Scandinavians: Grundtvig, Key, and Husén. Torsten Husén was born on 1 March 1916 in Lund, Sweden. In his roles as international researcher and institutional entrepreneur, he has manifested himself as one of the founding fathers of comparative and international education. In 1999, at the age of 83, he generously agreed to reflect on the past, present, and future of comparative education issues. But this book actually began some years earlier.

At the beginning of 1996, the University of Oslo's International Department invited faculties to apply for grants to invite foreign scholars for short visits to the university. An application to fund a one-month stay for Torsten Husén was accepted, and Husén was a visiting professor at the Institute for Educational Research in August 1996. A number of his lectures and many hours of interviews were taped, and the tapes later were transcribed by Conceincao Lorentzen. Between that period and 1999 I continued to communicate with Husén by mail. We also met for discussions in Stockholm. Out of all of these activities this book has now emerged.

I am grateful not only to the University of Oslo for the initial grant but also to the Institute for Educational Research, which generously provided additional financial support; to the Sweden Tercentenary Bank Foundation for their financial contribution to offset publication costs; and to the Phi Delta Kappa Educational Foundation for undertaking this project.

I want to thank Conceincao Lorentzen for her transcriptions and typing assistance and University of Oslo student Taran M.T. Thune for creative editorial assistance. Finally, I want to thank Torsten Husén for giving generously of his time to permit this work to be crafted. He also provided all of the photographs from his personal collection.

Part One
PAST

Roots of Academic Interests, 1940-1970

In organizing this work I have attempted to identify three periods, which I have labeled past, present, and future. The first of these, though it begins with Husén's childhood, concentrates roughly on the period from 1940 to 1970 and traces the roots of Husén's academic interests. The second, which I have termed "Present," extends from approximately 1971 to 1996, when this present work was begun. That period focuses on international education trends. Finally, the third period, "Future," attempts to capture Husén's thoughts about global education trends as they appear at the beginning of the new century.

Sociocultural and Academic Roots

Did you go to kindergarten?

No, I grew up in a small town of 800 inhabitants. There were two primary schools, one for the first two grades and another for the last four grades, and 40 to 60 children in each school. That's why I have such a preference for small schools.

And you went to school every day?

Yes, I went to school every day, but there were two grades in each class. I had two teachers, and these teachers had two and four grades each. I was six and the youngest in my class when I entered school. I don't know why my parents wanted me to start when I was six. On top of it, I started several weeks later than the

3

rest of them because I had had diphtheria and had been isolated for a couple of months. The school started on the 1st of September, but I did not start before the 1st of October.

Were you the oldest child in your family?

I was the oldest of four. My classmates had already started to learn to write some characters. I told the teacher I didn't need to learn handwriting because my father had an old Remington typewriter. I had learned to write by using my two index fingers to operate it. I said there was no point for me to learn handwriting; I used the typewriter. Anyhow, I had to take some extra lessons from the teacher to learn to read. You will find an account of this in my autobiography, *An Incurable Academic* (1983).

When you look back on your years in primary school, what was your most pleasant experience?

Well, I can't say that there is any particular recollection that stands out against the others. The first two years I had, as we call it in Swedish, a *småskolelærare*, a teacher specializing in only the first two grades. After that I had the same teacher for the next four grades. Primary mandatory schooling in Sweden at that time was six years. The teacher's name was Gustafsson, and in my view he was a very good teacher. He also was very active in municipal affairs. He may have been associated with the Liberal Party, but I do not think he was a politician. He was an active participant in municipal bodies of various kinds, and he knew all the parents. He correlated what he told us in the classroom, say in biology, to issues around us. In social studies he did the same. I have a very positive recollection of these four years with him.

Do you think he saw you as a particularly clever student?

Well, he didn't tell me, but he told my parents that he regarded me as the most well-educated, the one who had the widest horizon in terms of knowledge. I was a very active reader. I still remember when we came to grade three, we got particular textbooks — Grimberg's history — and we got one in natural sciences and one in geography. The one in history, by Grimberg, I still remember well. My interest in history had this particular connection, which is important to mention.

My father, who was a farm boy, had only 540 days of schooling. He grew up in the rural area and went to school for six years, but only half time. He and his brother took turns looking after the cattle at home. My mother, however, had eight years of girls school on the top of the primary grades; so she had 11 years of schooling. She had taken German and French. After she left school, she was trained as a telegrapher and subsequently was employed in the public telecommunication services in Sweden. She had a brother who took his doctorate in law at the same time as Gunnar Myrdal took his in Stockholm. So she had, of course, the idea that I should widen my horizon. Among other books she bought Grimberg's history, titled *The Wonderful Destiny of the Swedish People* (*Svenska Folkets Underbara Øden*), in nine volumes. I read them all at an early age.

Comparing your mother and father in these years of primary schooling, whom do you think had the most effect on your educational development at this time?

My mother without any doubt, even though my father was very education-minded. When he reached the age of 20, he attended a school of accounting that added something to his education, but my mother was the one who had the greater effect.

My mother's father was headmaster of the Manilla School for the "deaf and dumb" in Stockholm. His father was a primary school teacher in Skåne in southern Sweden. My maternal grandfather, the headmaster, did not complete a basic degree at the Lund University, but spent two or three years there before becoming a teacher. It was unusual at that time for somebody who had taken the matriculation examination for university entrance to become a primary school teacher. Ninety-nine percent of the teachers at primary level went through the *seminarium*, the teacher training seminar.

In 1929 a young Torsten Husén posed with his younger brother and sisters.

Torsten (left) poses with his father and younger brother in 1930.

Torsten is shown in this formal portrait on graduating from realskola *in 1932.*

Nineteen-year-old Torsten graduated from upper secondary school in 1935.

My paternal grandfather had been approached by the parish priest, who suggested that my father should be given an opportunity to go further, but that was economically impossible. My grandfather was a tenant farmer for one of the farms belonging to the University in Uppsala. But my father had, in a way, a very romantic conception of university studies. When he completed his schooling as an accountant, he went to Ultuna. Ultuna is now the Swedish Agricultural University, but at that time it was an Agricultural Institute. My father was keeping the institute's books, and the location was a few kilometers south of Uppsala. He used to go into Uppsala on first of May when people celebrated spring in the Botanic Gardens. They paid one or two Swedish crowns and then could drink as much punch as they wished. That was his kind of glamorous conception of university life in Uppsala.

You have given me the impression that your primary school teacher, Mr. Gustafsson, was an exceptional person. How do you now assess his influence on you?

I thought of him as supportive and encouraging. But it has occurred to me that there were several classmates who were discouraged by him. He thought they were hopeless, many of them coming from a culturally poor background. We were 43 in the class. In the third grade, I will say, according to some kind of social classification, at least 35 of them were from working-class or farm homes. The rest of us, including Gustafsson's own daughter, who was in the same grade, were some kind of middle class. I never felt wholeheartedly that Mr. Gustafsson was encouraging me, but I had the impression that we were in good touch with each other; and I heard through my mother, who probably asked him several times, that he appreciated the intellectual interest I had shown.

Moving on to secondary school, how was that experience?

Well, first let me tell you that I went to two secondary schools. First I went to the middle school [lower secondary school, or *realskola*] in Alvesta, 15 kilometers north of the little town where I grew up. There I took my *realexamen*, as they called it. From there, I went to three years of upper secondary school at the *real gymnasium* in Växjö.

How long were you in the realskola?

Four years. But during three of the four years I didn't make much effort at all. I had to go by train every day to the school. So I ate porridge very rapidly in the mornings and rushed to the train. I brought a sandwich and a bottle of milk with me; that was what I had for lunch. Three days a week I came back at three o'clock, and then I could eat. My family tried to keep a little bit of food warm from dinner. Dinner was really at noon. The three other days a week I came home at seven o'clock in the evening, which meant that I had no warm food since early in the morning. That in itself didn't keep me in good shape physically.

In Växjö, when attending the upper three years of secondary level, I lived with the family of a primary school teacher who, before he came to the teacher training seminar, had been a farm worker. I was well taken care of by this family. I had a room overlooking the dome and the old Växjö Gymnasium. The school was founded in 1643. It was the second in Sweden and had a long tradition. There were excellent teachers at the *gymnasium* level. Several of them had taken doctoral degrees.

The teacher I had in Swedish was also my teacher in history. His name was Rundquist. He played a very important role. First of all he widened my horizon; and when I had taken the matriculation exam, he recommended me strongly for a scholarship to the university. It was not really a scholarship. In fact, it was an interest-free loan. But I was fortunate to be one of the very few who got this support. It was 1,000 Swedish crowns the first year, then it increased to 1,200 crowns. This fortunate circumstance played an important role for my future.

So you owe this to your head teacher?

Yes, Mr. Rundquist was the one who widened my horizon. He played the same role at the *gymnasium* level as Gustafsson had done at the primary school level. I cannot remember a single occasion when Rundquist had to tell the pupils how to behave or had to restore order in the classroom — not a single occasion during those three years.

The three years in the gymnasium *were a good time for you?*

I finished the *real gymnasium* and took the university entrance exam. I have forgotten whether I had the highest grade-point average in my class or if it was somebody else. But anyhow, at that level it was taken for granted that I should try to enter the highly selective Royal Institute of Technology in Stockholm to become a civil engineer. But I didn't have the feeling that I was suited to be an engineer. Furthermore, I was only 19 years old and hadn't had any practice in an enterprise, which they normally put great emphasis on as an admission requirement. In order to see to it that I was not admitted to the Institute of Technology, I applied for the section on technical chemistry. There were only 20 that could be admitted and I think three or four hundred who applied. So I was not admitted. After that I decided to go to Lund, in order to take advantage of the rich intellectual smorgasbord at the university.

What subjects did you choose there?

Well, I took everything, so to speak. Despite the fact that I had not taken the humanistic or the classical program in the *gymnasium*, I began with history and philosophy. And in order to at least document my mathematical competence, after two months in Lund I took an exam in mathematics. Thus I had mathematics in my record before taking the "real stuff."

Before going to Lund in September 1935, I spent a couple of weeks in Poland, Germany, and Lithuania with my father. My father was then in the lumber business. He was sent to buy timber in Poland, but he had no knowledge of foreign languages; and my

German was rather fluent. In 1934 I had been sent to a family in Germany after the Nazis had taken over. But that family was close to the *Bekenntniskirche*. The mother of the family was the leader of that religious group, which resisted the Nazi regime. I could draw on this competence in German many years later in a two-month workshop in Frankfurt in 1952 on reconstructing the German education system.

Anyway, when I came to Lund I studied history, philosophy, and mathematics.

So you started with a number of subjects, but later you turned to psychology?

This was due to one of those exigencies in life that one cannot control. At that time in Sweden we had a system with university professors serving as external examiners, "censors," in the final exams in the upper secondary school. One of these examiners, whom I had encountered in Växjö, was John Landquist. He was a remarkable person, who might easily have held a professorship in literature. He edited all of Strindberg's writings, and he took his Ph.D. in philosophy. The title of his doctoral thesis was *Viljan* (*The Will*). He was talking to the three of us — we were divided in groups of two or three at the examination — and he took over the examination from our teacher. When I heard that he was appointed professor in Lund, I said to myself that I would like to study with such an inspiring person. His professorship was in education psychology, which he started in January of 1936 with a basic course in education history and theory. I remember this time very vividly and have described it in an essay in a book called *Encounters with Psychologists, Educators, and Others* (1992).

In order to take a master's degree (*magistergrad*) you had to take a basic course in education theory and history. He gave this. But I decided to go ahead with education psychology at more advanced levels. So in 1937 I took what was called the *Laudatur* course, the highest undergraduate course, given by Professor Landquist. Then I began to attend his advanced seminar. In

December 1937 he told me he needed an assistant, an amanuensis, and asked whether I would be interested. I had a sleepless night because I had already started to attend another series of advanced seminars by Lauritz Weibull, who was a professor of history. The two professors had to decide whether I should be "derailed" from history. Landquist was, as a humanist, also oriented toward history. Anyhow, it meant changing to another university discipline. This position would pay a salary of 150 Swedish crowns a month, which was more than I got from the interest-free loan. I realized that I would, if things worked out successfully, not have any sizable debts to pay off when I finished my studies. So I became Landquist's assistant in 1938 and continued until I took my doctorate in 1944.

In 1941 I took my licentiate degree. The graduate studies were organized in two steps. At the graduate level, we had the licentiate exam, which took, if you worked full time, about three years. On top of that, you had to write your doctoral thesis, which had to be printed and submitted in 330 copies. Thus the idea was that it should take at least five years after the bachelor's degree. But in most cases it took much longer because most graduate students had to spend time earning their living.

In 1942 Torsten Husén was a research assistant at Lund University.

You did your degree work rather rapidly.

I did it from 1938 to 1944, and during that time I also took courses in the history of literature and had military service for two years. But I was fortunate, because I was able to collect the data for my doctoral thesis during my service at the Army Staff in 1941-43. From the fall of 1939 to the fall of 1940, practically for one year, I served in the artillery as a regular soldier. But then I got in touch with a person who was a major at the War College in Stockholm, Ericsson. When he heard that I had a licentiate in psychology, he said, "Why don't we use you in preparing a system of military aptitude tests?" He had the idea that this should be done. They had seen this in Germany. Later on they also got information through the military attachés on how it was done in Britain and in the United States, but the Germans had developed this already in the 1930s. I spent three months in 1941 in Stockholm at the so-called Gray House, the military headquarters, writing up memoranda on how one could introduce aptitude tests. I had to use various sources of information, official and unofficial, about what was done in the countries at war. We got particular information through the Swedish military attachés.

The memorandum was submitted to Per Edvin Sköld, the famous Swedish politician, who was the minister of defense at the time. Per Edvin Sköld was an extremely interesting person, by the way. He decided that one should introduce intelligence testing at the induction in Sweden, so that all those who were inducted into the military service could be classified according to their IQ. Soon they began to consider a special testing program for those who were applying as pilots in the Swedish Air Force. So, in July 1942 I was hired as a consultant, half time with the Army Staff, which meant that I was traveling back and forth between Lund and Stockholm. In the fall of 1942 I began to collect data that I could use for a doctoral thesis.

It is fair to say that the war and the military's need for competence in applied psychology had a decisive influence on your academic career?

It had a very strong influence on me. On 1 July 1944 I was employed as a regular member of the Army staff. This was just a few months before my doctoral defense.

Did you have a military rank as an officer?

No, I didn't. I was not very keen on having a military rank. I think I was a corporal when I finished my military career.

I moved to Stockholm in 1944. We began to evaluate pilots in the Swedish air force by means of a thorough two-day testing program. Until 1948 my title was military psychologist.

During that period I had close contact with colleagues in Norway. In November 1946 I was in Oslo. The Norwegian Supreme Commander then was General Hanson. He chaired a committee preparing something in the field of military psychology similar to what we had in Sweden, to test and classify everybody inducted into the military service. The Norwegian defense's department of psychology was then established. A lieutenant colonel from Stockholm accompanied me, and we spent a week or so in Oslo and established close contact. My Norwegian counterpart was Vidkun Coucheron Jarl. This was a very hectic period in my life.

Was it your familiarity with Germany that stimulated your interest in psychology?

Not necessarily. German psychology was very influential internationally. The American pioneers in education psychology had all been trained in Germany, for example, Stanley Hall and Charles Judd in Chicago. I wrote about this in the *International Encyclopedia of Education*, by the way. The German influence was strong, academically through the Wundt experimental laboratory in 1879 in Leipzig, and you had George Elias Mueller in Göttingen. David Katz, who escaped from Germany to Sweden in the 1930s, became a professor of psychology in Stockholm. He was a student of Mueller. During World War I German experimental psychologists had started to apply psychology in military personnel selection.

Would you go as far as saying that Germany was a sort of leader in applied military psychology before World War II?

The Americans also had started this. Walter Bingham at the Carnegie Institute of Technology was involved. These people were the second generation in the United States. The first generation was at the turn of the century. Most of the Ph.D.s in psychology and adjacent disciplines had then been taken in Germany. German universities had something that didn't exist in the United States at that time — the Humboldtian idea of integrating research and academic teaching.

Was your mentor, Professor Landquist, influenced by the Germans?

Yes, though this was not his field in particular. He was a humanist, and I was more a technologist, if you wish.

You stayed in touch for a long time?

Oh yes, I had the last letter from him in 1974. I had written to him about something when I was at the Stanford "think tank" from 1973 to 1974. I think that was the last correspondence with him. He was then 93 years old. He had a heart attack and died in the spring of 1974.

Speaking about your affiliation with the discipline of psychology, what was your relation to psychoanalysis?

Well, it's important to mention that Landquist was the one who introduced psychoanalysis in Sweden. He wrote a book in 1916 about Gustav Frøding, the Swedish poet, which was to some extent a psychoanalytic study. He used a psychoanalytical approach in analyzing Frøding's personality. Then in 1918-19 Landquist visited Vienna with his wife, Elin Wägner. She was one of the leading feminists in Sweden and also a leading person in "Save the Children." There was starvation in Vienna. Landquist took advantage of the opportunity, because he accompanied Elin, to visit Freud. Landquist decided to translate two of Freud's important books into Swedish in the 1920s. In the 1930s I attended several seminars related to psychoanalysis at Lund University.

How did this experience relate to your interview with Freud?

I did not have an interview with him in the proper sense of the word. I got in contact with Karl Bühler. He had written a book, *Sprachtheorie*, that came out in 1934. Unfortunately it was in German, and this made it difficult for English-speaking readers to understand what kind of pioneering work this book was.

He was the husband of Charlotte.

Yes, Charlotte was 10 years younger than Karl. I visited Karl Bühler for a few days in Vienna in 1937. When I told Landquist that I was going to Vienna, he wrote a letter of introduction for me. He said that I should try to meet Freud. He knew that Freud was ill with throat cancer by that time. I went to Bergstrasse 19 with my letter of introduction and showed it to the housekeeper who opened the door. I asked if it would be possible to meet Professor Freud, and she said she would ask the professor. She came back and said that I could come back the next day at 10 o'clock. When I came back she told me that I should not bother him too long. His disease impaired his ability to carry on a conversation, but I think I talked to him maybe for 20 minutes or so. The only thing I remember is that he felt his former students, I wouldn't use the word "betrayed," but they had turned against him.

Psychoanalysts widened my horizon. They made me understand the enormous influence that psychoanalysis had in Norway. I knew Harald Schelderup very well. He asked me to "sit" on his chair at Oslo University for a year or two in 1950-1951. He wanted to take a leave of absence from his professorship to write a monograph distilling his experiences in psychoanalysis. I still remember visiting him when he lived at Lysaker. He was a very keen professional. I think Vidkun Coucheron Jarl was the one who suggested that he turn to me. But going to Oslo meant such a deviation from what I was doing in Stockholm. After having thought about it thoroughly, I had to thank him but say that I could not accept.

Leaving psychoanalysis as a particular field, your list of publications indicates a thorough interest in adolescence and the psychology of this development phase. Why?

I have to tell you that I didn't feel very happy during my own adolescence. This applied in particular to the four years I talked about previously, while attending middle school from the age of 12 or 13 up to age 16. I didn't mention that I was not very happy with the teaching climate in that school. They did not have very good teachers. I was probably regarded by my classmates as a funny fellow who had, in certain respects, other interests than the rest of them. There was also some kind of bullying.

So this period interested me when I collected data from 6,000 young men who were applying for permanent positions in the Swedish military. The youngest were 16; the median age was 18. I used the same terminology as Charlotte Bühler. She divided the years 12 to 20 into two periods: puberty, which was the period when the physical change took place, and adolescence, the period of psychological maturity, or *Kulturpubertät* she called it. I had a particular interest in looking into the social relations: What kind of relations did young people have to their parents, to their school environment (including teachers), and to their classmates? Furthermore, I was interested in the leisure-time interests they had and what they were reading. All this was dealt with in my thesis.

So was part of your motivation for the topic of your doctoral thesis your own adolescent experience?

Yes, I think many of us who then went on to more advanced studies in psychology were at least partly motivated by trying to solve our own problems.

Within the field of adolescent psychology, were you interested in measuring intelligence?

Well, I was completely incompetent in terms of intelligence testing or psychometrics, not to speak about the statistical paraphernalia. But I worked with one of my friends in Landquist's

17

advanced seminar, Siver Hallgren, who was a teacher in Malmø. He wanted to write a licentiate thesis on IQ and social background. Today this is an extremely trivial problem, but at that time the issue was unexplored. There were very few or no studies. Second, everybody thought that IQ was inherited. It was there, and it could not be changed very much. Hallgren had the idea of conducting a survey of all the 10-year-olds born in 1928 in Malmø by using a group intelligence test and background questionnaire. There were about 1,600 10-year-olds, almost all in third grade. Hallgren chose the third grade because in the fourth grade it was possible to transfer to the *realskola*.

Was this the beginning of the famous Malmø Longitudinal Study?

Yes. The study started in 1937. Hallgren needed some assistance, so I became a little involved in the preparation of the study and in the data collection. The testing took place in 1938. The test scores were correlated with background factors, school marks, and ratings by the teachers. There were four sets of factors then: test scores, family background, school marks, and the information about whether they had special education or had been helped by the social services, such as getting free clothing and free books or things of that sort. I followed the planning of this project as a participant in Landquist's seminar. When Hallgren was ready with his licentiate thesis, Landquist asked me to serve as a kind of "opponent." It was not a formal defense, but I learned quite a lot.

That task constituted my training course for becoming a testmaker because Hallgren himself devised and standardized the test that was used. He was in contact with John Elmgren, who at that time was a professor in Gothenburg. Elmgren had been trained by Jaederholm, a testing pioneer in Sweden, who had been trained in London at Francis Galton's laboratory.

The work for this study took place from 1937 through the spring semester of 1939. Hallgren later did a small follow-up of those who went to the *realskola*. These results were published in 1943 in a book called *Group Testing (Grupptestning)*.

In 1948, when I was in charge of military testing in Sweden, the Malmø students were 20 years old. So half of the third-graders, roughly 800 boys, would be inducted into military service. In relation to this they could be tested, and information about their careers after they left school could be collected. The great majority had only seven years of schooling. This was the mandatory minimum for three-quarters of them. I decided to locate them; and when they were inducted to military service, they had to fill in questionnaires about what they had done after leaving school. I published this study in a book called *The Predictive Value of Test Scores* (*Testresultatens Prognosvärde*), which came out in 1950. I also wrote an article called "The Influence of Schooling upon IQ," which was not published in a psychological journal, but in a philosophical one called *Theoria* in Lund in 1951.

I tried to convince Sivert Hallgren that he should do a follow-up, and we continued discussing this in the early 1950s. Then he became ill and passed away. Before that, he sent me the data cards, one for each individual, so I had these cards in my office. In 1964 I recruited a young research assistant to help me do the follow-up. He was later to be my successor, Ingemar Fägerlind. We began in the mid-1960s to collect further information. At that time the Malmø cohort was 36 years old. A book reporting the results was published in 1969, called *Talent, Opportunity, and Career*.

Was Professor Landquist's attitude about this kind of testing positive?

He was critical about it and the reliance on it. In his lectures he was very critical about intelligence testing but without denying that it was a complementary part of the psychological mapping, so to speak. Credibility was kept to a reasonable level, and in my case it was an introduction to "selling" the idea of what was later referred to as the "reserve of ability." That was the next big project I was involved in.

Speaking about test psychology, were you influenced by Skinner's approach?

He did not have any influence on me in the early times we are talking about now. Later I was very close to Fred and Eve Skinner. When they visited Europe in 1948, my wife and I met them; and then they visited us in Stockholm in 1961. I wrote about Skinner in *Encounters*, which I referred to earlier. The longest essay is about him. We usually avoided speaking about psychology when we met because we had other common interests, philosophy, music, and literature among them. Skinner wrote a couple of novels and in his youth intended to become a writer of fiction. I met him with Ingrid as late as in 1987. He was then 83 years old, and he gave us a book titled *Enjoy Old Age*. He wrote a nice dedication on the first page: "To Ingrid and Torsten, for future use, from Fred."

In the early days, Landquist was a very strong adversary, denouncing behaviorism. As a young 20-year-old student I even wrote a seminar paper criticizing behaviorism. I was much more influenced by German psychologists, such as Dilthey, and their holistic and gestalt approaches.

Summing up these recollections from the field of psychology, what sort of psychologist did you become? You are not a behaviorist; you are not a psychoanalyst. How would you describe your position within the discipline?

I was for many years, from 1941 through 1952, mainly involved in military psychology. But I did not run this kind of mechanical testing myself. Others administered the group tests. I personally interviewed hundreds and hundreds of prospective officer candidates. I wrote the interview instructions for my colleagues because I was in charge of the whole operation. It was a kind of personality psychology that grew up under the influence of Landquist and a Finnish psychologist with whom I got in touch early and who influenced me. His name was Eino Kaila. He had been in Vienna and was strongly influenced both by the psychologists and by the Vienna circle of philosophers. It was a psychology emphasizing the "holistic" approach. The psychoanalytic approach also was included by putting emphasis on what happened during the first few years of life. I also was emphasizing the dynamics of the psychological development processes.

Do you have a leaning toward humanist psychology?

Yes, in spite of the many elements of psychometrics that went into it. I was by no means sworn to the mechanistic approach. I got to know Thurstone, the American psychologist, who, by the way, was of Swedish background. His parents came from Sweden and emigrated to the United States. Tunstrøm was their Swedish name. Thurstone went to school in Stockholm. He understood Swedish, but I never heard him speak it. He originally was trained as an engineer. He worked with Edison and was involved in improving the film camera. But then Walter Bingham, who was at the Carnegie Institute of Technology, persuaded him to move into psychology. He went to Chicago and took his Ph.D. there. We had Thurstone as a visiting professor in Stockholm for a full year in the early 1950s. He was regarded as the big name in psychometrics. Factor analysis was one of the most sophisticated techniques you could use.

From your recollections up to now, would it be fair to think that your academic identity would be that of a psychologist? But then, knowing what you have done later in your career in the field of comparative education, I would like to challenge you on this point.

Well, it is difficult. I have perhaps been drawing on too many sources. With regard to identity, I feel like a social science generalist. I have been called on to serve as an expert when it came to establishing a professorship in sociology at Stockholm University. I have tried to keep my horizon broad, which is, of course, impossible nowadays. I have tried to stretch it as far as I could. However, provincialism sometimes strikes me as a professional disease among people in education. It applies to education in general. It plagues the teachers, but it also applies to quite a few education researchers both in America and Europe. They are not internationally oriented and have rather narrow horizons.

When I first moved into education, I got in touch with UNESCO. I was reminded of this a few months ago, when UNESCO asked me to write a personal memoir of contacts with that organization. UNESCO was founded in 1946 in London. In 1948 I got in touch with Otto Klineberg and Hadley Cantril, two social psychologists who were hired by UNESCO. A next step was to become involved when it set up international committees of primary and secondary school curriculum, respectively, in the mid-1950s. So I frequently went to Paris in the 1950s.

UNESCO had the idea, at least those who were in charge of the education department, that it should try to establish some kind of universal principles that could be applied in developing curricula at the primary and secondary level. It was perhaps a rather naive conception that curricula could be developed according to some universal principles. But it opened up an international aspect to education problems. This started in the 1950s and early 1960s and contributed somewhat to the establishment of comparative and international education.

Several things happened at that time. In 1952 UNESCO established an institute of education in Hamburg. A Norwegian by the name of Langeland became the first director. He was very useful in setting the institute operating in the right direction. Then you had people like Theodore Schultz in Chicago and Arthur Lewis at Princeton. They later shared a Nobel Prize. They and some European colleagues began to look at education as an investment in human capital. And we began to discuss how to implement international aspirations in the established education systems by founding the international bureau of education in Geneva. Education research was conducted in various European countries. One began to look at what they are doing now and then. So when all of these circumstances came together around 1960, the Comparative Education Society for Europe was established. I was one of the "founding fathers." We got together in Hamburg in 1960 and in London in 1961. We had a congress of the new Comparative Education Society in Amsterdam in 1962. In 1970 I became chairman of the governing board of the International Institute for

Educational Planning (IIEP) in Paris, which I had been involved in setting up in 1963. All of this, in my case, made me emphasize the international dimension of education. Then in 1980, I was invited to serve as editor-in-chief, along with Neville Postlethwaithe, of *The International Encyclopedia of Education*, which was another major international endeavor. We prepared a second edition during the early 1990s.

All this taken together has created your identity as an international education researcher.

Yes. Coming back to what I said a while ago, I feel very strongly that too many educators suffer from provincialism. They think that what is happening with students is what is happening only in their particular classroom, disregarding the cultural and social setting of education enterprises.

What do you think triggered this international orientation of yours?

It is difficult to say. As a social science researcher, I was eager to widen the horizon. But there are certain experiences. For instance, during my first years as a professor I received a grant to visit the United States for two months. I used the summer vacation to do this. My wife and I went together, but we deserted our three children. I wrote about this in an essay called "A Journey in American Education" (1955).

When did this journey take place?

In 1954. We started out in Michigan, at the State University of Michigan. Then we went to the University of Illinois and from Illinois to Washington, D.C. After that we went to North Carolina, and finally we had a three-week stay at Columbia University Teachers College.

At that time had you already been to Germany and become acquainted with American colleagues there?

23

In the summer of 1952 the whole family went to Germany. There was a seven-week workshop organized by the American High Commissioner in Frankfurt. I was called to it at the end. They had the idea that German professors of education needed an international injection. A multiplying effect was expected by bringing all of the professors of education together who were full professors (*Ordinarius*). There was only one full professor in each discipline at each university. There were only about 25 in all, and then you had some professors of the *pädagogische hochschulen*, the institutions of teacher education. Bringing them together and spending almost two months with colleagues from other countries would widen their horizons. From abroad there were six colleagues from the United States and six from European countries. Those of us who were European also were invited to bring an assistant. The whole exercise was extremely important in terms of promoting international exchange.

Was this your first main international participation?

Yes, I would say so. This was the first point of particular importance for what was going to happen later on in my career. I had, however, started to attend international congresses in psychology. The first one was held in Edinburgh in 1948, and the second one in Bern, Switzerland, in 1949. The second congress focused on applied psychology. The one in Edinburgh was about general psychology. Furthermore, there were two congresses in Sweden in 1951.

The Comprehensive School Movement

The comprehensive school movement has received particular attention in your research. To what extent do you think there were particular ideological and cultural preconditions in Scandinavia for this model of schooling?

There were several determinants behind this in the 1940s. Compulsory education in Sweden, as in other European countries, was beset with the problem that differentiation into types of schools took place after only four years of primary schooling. A small minority was diverted to an elite type of education, whereas the rest had to stay in primary school. I found that at the age of 11, 10% to 15% of the students were diverted into the more academic type of secondary education. Most of them came from a socially favorable background. There was a growing awareness that this parallel system of education was not the best one.

There also were purely ideological forces behind the comprehensive school movement. Particularly among the Social Democrats there was quite a lot of talk about "democratization" of advanced formal education. When I say advanced education, I also refer to the preparatory years on the academic track of the secondary school. In the first statistical survey conducted in the 1940s, it was discovered that the chance for a boy or a girl with a working-class background to go on to the university was one or maybe two percent. The chance for a boy or girl whose parents had higher education was 40% to 60%. If background was elevated economically, with parents who were employed in large companies, it was 60% to 70%. So this issue of democratizing upper secondary and higher education became a major political question. This was before the idea that came later, that in order to be more competitive in the world market, a country had to take care of its intellectual capital.

Anyhow, I became interested in this in 1945, when I began to analyze the data from the military induction testing. In the 1940s I had eight complete age groups of 20-year-old males, 50,000 a year. When I compared the distribution of test scores of those who went to the upper secondary school and took the matriculation examination with those who had only six years of primary education, there was quite a lot of overlap. This indicated the existence of a "reserve of ability." I don't know if you have heard about the so-called Stockholm study in the late 1950s. Nils-Eric Svensson, one of my graduate students, was in charge of this study. We followed up on all of those pupils who in 1954 were in grade four. Half of Stockholm had by then introduced the comprehensive school. In one-half of the city you could not leave primary school after grade four to go to the secondary one, you had to stay on. In the other half of the city it was possible to transfer. The main argument of those who were against the reform was that a majority of pupils were not able to profit from an academic type of secondary education. You had to have either different programs, different lines of studies — I call it line differentiation — or you had to differentiate within the class, which was even more difficult. I wrote a little book called *Problems of Differentiation in Swedish Compulsory Schooling* (1962), which was originally a series of lectures that I had given in 1959 as a visiting professor at the University of Chicago.

Why do you think there has been a particular Scandinavian drive for using schooling as a vehicle in the general democratization process?

Comprehensive schooling was a sequel to the welfare society. There was very little talk about this in the 1930s, when welfare reforms began to be introduced. There were all kinds of reforms of social security. After a certain level of economic safety had been guaranteed, it was thought that one also should introduce a system where education could profit from the improved standard of living. We had a school reform in Sweden in 1927, as you can see from my book about the *Problems of Differentiation*. In 1927 a compromise was struck, providing two possibilities. You could either go to six years of primary schooling and then go to the secondary, or you could transfer after four or five years of primary school to the academic secondary school.

And in which political form did this occur? Do you relate it more to Social Democratic or Liberal policies?

Well, there were both. The Liberals were the ones who invented the comprehensive idea, not the Social Democrats. Social Democrats were more for the material side of the matter. Around the turn of the century, it was Fridtjuv Berg who was of seminal value in the Swedish debate. Already in 1883 he spelled out the idea of primary school as basic schooling for all. He was the minister of education in two liberal governments at the beginning of the century. Thus it was originally one of the main ideas of the Liberal Party. As a matter of fact, the Liberal Fridtjuv Berg entered the parliament supported by a leading Social Democrat, Hjalmar Branting. The Social Democrats formed a very important part of the political background here. Politically these two parties were in line on education policy. But later on, in the 1950s and 1960s, the Liberals were a bit hesitant when it came to increasing compulsory education to nine years of common schooling.

At this time then, had the Social Democrats taken the lead?

They took the lead. I'll give you an example. By 1945 on average about 15% of an age group went on to secondary school. But the transfer was enormously dependent on the availability of secondary education, either municipal "middle school" or *realskola* (lower secondary level) or the *realskola* as part of the *læroverk/ gymnasium* (upper secondary). There were these three possibilities. But in the rural areas in northern Sweden the number of those who went on to the upper secondary, to the *gymnasium*, after the reform of 1962, increased tenfold over a period of a few years. This was because, in the first place, you had the first nine years of schooling, including three extra years of education required for entry to the *gymnasium*. So the school reform was of enormous importance for the whole system of education in Sweden. But it also contributed to the narrowing of the gaps between the social classes. In a period of less than 20 years the proportion of working-class boys who went on and took the matriculation exam qualifying for the university increased from 1% or 2% to 10%.

Which basic conditions prompted this strong motivation for extended education?

One should not underestimate the prestige it meant to have additional education. But, on the other hand, it meant certain sacrifices in terms of not having any income, even though some allowances could be given. Furthermore, because of the low wage and salary differences in Sweden, extra years of schooling no longer provided as much economic advantage.

How do you react to criticisms about the comprehensive education reform effecting a "brain drain" from the countryside and the working class?

More than fifty years ago, the director of ABF (the workers' study organization in Sweden) Gunnar Hirdman, was talking about the "fortunate injustice" that the working class didn't have access to advanced formal education. This meant that brain capacity could be preserved for the benefit for the working class. In certain homes it was regarded as a kind of treason against your own class if you went on with schooling and moved up the social ladder. It is important to remember the phenomenon that I have labeled "selective migration." Ejnar Neymark, who was in charge of vocational guidance in Sweden, took his Ph.D. with me in 1961. He looked at selective migration. He followed up on the young men who were tested at induction in 1948. Neymark found out that those who migrated had more frequently gone on to further education. I myself did the first studies on selective migration in the late 1940s. I could show that urbanization meant intellectual "brain drain" for the rural areas in Sweden, as well as in other countries. It was an enormous "brain drain" irrespective of what kind of criterion you were using, either IQ or school marks.

What do you think about the dilemma of the state trying to establish a common basis for education of everybody in the name of democracy, and at the same time creating a brain drain of the social classes (for example, trade unions)?

During the 1950s I participated in conferences that the Swedish Central Federation of Trade Unions (LO) was organizing. I learned to know these very brilliant people, who were educated almost entirely within the labor movement, and who, if they had been born in other families further up the social ladder, would

28

have become academics, professors, or head administrators. They were able to use their "self-education" both as members of Parliament and in the preparation of the labor movement. But you are hinting at something that I wrote about just a few weeks ago, namely "Equalizing Education: A Democratic Dilemma" (in *Insights and Opinions About the Learning Society*, 1999). The dilemma is that everybody has the opportunity, which my friend Michael Young described in his book about meritocracy. Since he wrote this work, there has been some empirical evidence supporting his thesis that the system favors those with the most able genes.

You have written about the "qualification pyramid." What does this mean?

I used the symbol of a pyramid in describing the structure of formal education qualifications. I have written about the change from a pyramid to an egg. In one of my early publications, the pyramid had 60% to 70% at the bottom in primary education, and then 20% to 25% in secondary education, finally a maximum of 5% in tertiary education. The system can now be described as an "egg," but the egg is placed on its tip. There is now a new underclass of 10% to 15% who have failed miserably, and then the remaining 85% to 90% have more or less succeeded.

Earlier we talked about the differentiation problem. How would you differentiate secondary school students with diverse backgrounds so that all work happily together?

It is quite evident that this problem hasn't been solved, in spite of all good intentions. Among others, the secretary of the 1946 Swedish school commission, Arvidson, thought that the individualization of teaching within the framework of the classroom would be the solution. But this has not been the case. The prevailing approach in the classroom is still "frontal instruction" and sprinkling wisdom evenly over the whole class. Individualization requires enormous preparation. In a country like China I have noticed, particularly in the so-called key schools, that science teachers or mathematics teachers were available to give only three lessons a day. But they are required to prepare, for themselves and the students, working material and working plans. Thus they are certainly working hard, but they spend only three hours in the classroom. The rest is preparation and evaluation. I mean this is what the teachers are saying, and my impression is that it is so, particularly in the *gymnasium.*

The *gymnasium* is the next level in Sweden where we will soon have almost 100% of the students. That it doesn't work is neither good for those who are behind nor for those who need more stimulation in order to work. I hate to put it in such general terms, but I think this pretty well states the problem. We have not been able to reform teacher education or schedule teaching loads according to the Chinese practice. Differentiation may be organized through offering more advanced courses and less advanced courses that can be taken in the same classroom.

Moving the perspective from Chinese key schools to everyday Scandinavian education, which do you think would be better, to keep all students in the same classroom or to separate them?

I think they have to be separated, in different classrooms with different teachers. Another thing that has happened is that homework has been more and more reduced. I don't know how it is in Norway, but in Sweden this is quite evident, just as in the United States. Harold Stevenson from the University of Wisconsin has conducted empirical studies along with teams in the United States, Japan, Taiwan, and China. They also have had the experience that very little homework is required in the United States as compared to the other three countries. This is something we have to think about. There was among those promoting reforms in Sweden a resistance to homework, because they said it favored those who come from homes where the parents were better educated and where the kids will get more help. I think they have not considered the consequences of such an attitude.

Has there been a change in parents' attitudes toward education in general in Scandinavia during the last 40 years?

I have even more than 40 years' perspective. If you look into my bibliography, you'll find that in the 1950s I conducted a study commissioned by the school board of the city of Stockholm on the school-home relationship. It was a very good study, but I will not take credit for it. My brother Lennart, who was then a teacher in Stockholm, was the one who was doing most of the thinking before we conducted the data collection. I mean, he came up with the theory behind it. Sixten Marklund also participated; he did a parallel study in Luleå. What we did was develop an attitude scale on matters of education, how authoritarian or non-authoritarian parents and teachers were. We administered this instrument to the teachers and the parents. We interviewed the parents as well, and found out that the greater the discrepancy between parents and teachers, the more difficult it was for the children in school.

What has happened since 1955, when we collected data and reported our study, is that the number of mothers with children of school age that are working outside the home went from less than 20% to almost 80%. The number of divorces tripled or quadrupled over the same period, and the number of children per family went down. Then there has been an influx of people from the rural areas to the cities. This is an enormous change to the setting in which education, either at home or in school, occurs and is important to have in mind.

There was a public debate between conservatives and liberals about the problem of differentiation. How do you assess their arguments?

The conservatives were not objecting to equality; you cannot do that explicitly nowadays. But they were objecting to the change because of pedagogical difficulties. You cannot have all the students in the same classroom, simply because some of them easily absorb what is taught and some do not. This was the main objection, both by the conservatives and the teachers. But you also have another thing here, the unspoken "elitism." As long as you have a selective system, those who gain from it are, of course, for it; and those who are losing out are against. It is as simple as that.

31

Today we do not have the social or economic situation we had at that time, so it is a bit unfair to try to assess the past within today's reality. At that time, you had on the average greater differentiation of formal education among the parents. Those who now have children in school were born in the 1940s, 1950s, or 1960s. Of the parents in the mid-1950s to the early 1960s, up to 75% had only primary education. The differences in home background in terms of parental education were much wider than they are now.

Do you think the conditions for benefiting from schooling have changed?

Yes. This is one thing that I have been coming back to over and over again: People nowadays tend to discuss problems of school education as if we were still living in the 1950s. I dealt with this issue in a book titled *What Has Happened to the School?* (1987).

So what you are saying implies that with education analyses we always need to be aware of historical and socioeconomic conditions?

Yes, that is what I have been talking about with both teachers and candidates and to other groups. Irrespective of what you do in the classroom, or with the system, you cannot disregard the socioeconomic setting of education.

In your writings you have used the terms "the youth revolt" and "the crisis." When did you first start talking about this?

I came out with a book in 1972 called *The School's Crisis*. I was then aware of what was happening. The changes in socioeconomic conditions for education, the massification, the rising costs, and the crises that had to do with changes some politicians thought they were able to implement in a short time.

I have not written very much about the youth revolt. James Coleman and I wrote a book together for OECD, titled *Becoming Adult in a Changing Society* (1985). The reason we were asked to write the book, and I'm talking now about the late 1970s and early 1980s, was the rising youth unemployment. Until then there was very little youth unemployment in most European countries and the United States. But one problem we pointed out was a growing tendency for there to be no place for young people in society until they were about 20 to 25. They are in formal training or whatever, and there are no jobs for them. This long period of adolescence makes it frustrating for them. Yesterday I saw on television a report from Stockholm where half of those between 17 and 25 do not have a steady job. Twenty years ago this figure was something around 20%.

The crisis in the school, however, is the increased burden put on formal education over the last few decades. In the first place, the number of years in school has increased, as well as the number of young people in school. There is, of course, a demographic aspect to this. This is something that is always lacking in education planning, attempts to foresee how many teachers are needed five to 10 years ahead. Such predictions have been lacking outside Scandinavia as well. Georg Picht, who was on the board of the Max Planck Institute in Berlin, wrote a book in 1964 called *Die Deutsche Bildungskatastrophe* (*The German Education Catastrophe*). He pointed out that over the next few years there would be a need for an enormous increase of teachers. No planning had been done in Germany at the federal level, but he had been working with some people from OECD trying to predict how many teachers would be needed. After the war there was an enormous baby boom in Germany. He showed that, if over the next few years all who took the matriculation exam and thereby qualified for higher education became teachers, it still wouldn't suffice to cover the need for teachers. I still remember the shock that Willy Brandt and his government experienced when they became aware of this. They knew how many kids were born during a given year but were not projecting this over a decade or more. The government took very drastic measures. They doubled or tripled the capacity of the teacher training institutions. This took time, of course; you cannot do it overnight. Simultaneously as they were doing this, there was a strong downward trend in the fertility rate in Germany. This led to unemployment among teachers 20 years later.

Thinking of Sweden or Scandinavia, I wonder if part of the crisis is the many students from different backgrounds, who earlier did not have the opportunity, now coming into a school they are not fit for culturally but are instrumentally motivated for, as an opportunity of moving up the social ladder?

The experience of schooling is, of course, part of the problem. Motivation is becoming, as we have described in the Academia Europea's *Schooling in Modern European Society* (1992), a major problem. There are now growing numbers of students in the secondary school who think that they are attending something meaningless. This is the case in all industrialized countries.

Aren't the Scandinavian countries trying to extend the comprehensive principle into the upper secondary school?

In Sweden we have until recently had a differentiated *gymnasium*. Some went there two years, some went three years. Those considered "practical" and heading for the vocations had, as a rule, two years of upper secondary schooling. Those heading for university had three years. But in the new *gymnasium* everybody has to spend three years. In certain core subject areas, like Swedish, everybody has the same courses. It is hypocritical to say that everybody has the same academic ability or that they are achieving the same. This spills over to the grading system and creates serious motivational problems.

Germany and Austria have long traditions of apprenticeship systems. At the age of 14 or 15 you can finish full-time schooling, you only take some 10 hours a week in school, and you spend the rest of your time in an enterprise where you are an apprentice. But you are still under compulsory schooling until you are 18. My impression, and what came out of international evaluations, is that this system has worked very well.

Let us go back to something we already have talked about, the family institution. Could you please point out what you see as the main changes in how the family reacts to the children's schooling?

Yes, we have another thing that I have not yet mentioned. I'm talking about the family as an institution, how it has changed in terms of mothers working outside the home. I'm not saying anything about working at home. It may be even more troublesome to work at home, but anyway the majority are now working outside the home. The number of divorces has increased. I have not mentioned another thing that relates to the school, namely parental commitment, which has been diminishing. This is what we have found in all highly industrialized countries. To an increasing extent the family does not involve itself in the school. In many instances it does not care at all.

This has to do with sociocultural background. More educated parents tend to be more involved. In the lower social classes there is a certain reluctance of involvement, because they think that the school does not care about them and their opinion. This also is reflected in the fact that it is difficult to establish local steering bodies where parents are involved. Denmark has a long tradition of parental steering bodies. When the former Swedish minister of education, Bengt Göransson, tried to introduce what was called local school boards, he ran into difficulties. In Chinatown in San Francisco, back in 1978, I talked to parents and learned that many of them were buying an extra set of textbooks in order to be able to help their children. There is a completely different commitment in the Asian countries, and you see now in the United States that children with Asian background are performing very well in international achievement testing.

We are talking about the middle or upper class being more interested in education. However, some people wonder whether the present urban middle class actually takes less interest in their children's schooling than this class did before?

I think that, on the whole, commitment to the school in modern society has diminished. Parents are so preoccupied with their own things. I cannot find any other explanation for it. There is no doubt that there is less commitment on the part of the family. It also has to do with the welfare society. It is expected that society at large should take the responsibility.

In writing about modernizing the school, you have dealt with the problem of the grading system. What's the trouble?

On the one hand, we do not want to acknowledge that we are living in a meritocracy. The better you achieve, the better your chances are to succeed in various ways. We once had a debate in Sweden where it was said that grading should be dropped because it did not fulfill any function. I said once that this is like a remedy you use in trying to cure the illness by removing what you can see on the skin. I mean that achievements have to be graded to be individually evaluated. I'm not referring here to the collective evaluation of a whole class or a school or school system.

So there is a dilemma here. Grading ought to be taken away because it shows differences between people. But on the other hand, there is a need to communicate the different competence of people.

Yes, it concerns selection for the next level in the education system. I think some system of grading is needed. Parents want it. It is said that it has detrimental repercussions on instruction. But it is even worse to take away grading; then nobody would care to absorb anything. If we could agree that it is necessary to grade, and I do not think that would be too difficult, then the technical problem of communicating the results would become easier. It is not easy as such, but it is easier than if you say it is not necessary to have a grading system.

Achievements in schools have become one of several trademarks connected to your research. What has happened to achievements in schools in different countries, earlier and now?

I would like to relate this to the establishment of IEA, the International Association for the Evaluation of Educational Achievement. This was about 1960, in the wake of what I used to refer to as the "Sputnik Psychosis." There was a need to find out what changed in the system in terms of student competence and how the students felt in that new system. We conducted the first IEA studies in mathematics. We began by trying out the instruments in 1961-62, collecting data in early 1964, and processing it in 1964-65. It was discovered that among the 13-year-olds in 12 countries, the best achievements were made in Japan. I have forgotten which one was at the bottom, either Sweden or the United States. I think the United States was at the bottom. At that time there were no comparisons over time. So in Sweden some were saying that this was an outcome of the school reform of 1962. In fact the new reform was passed by Parliament in 1962, so the first cohort began school in 1963 when the new curriculum was introduced. Thus, the study reflected the old system at best.

In the United States you had certain problems like poor teachers. We repeated the study in mathematics in the late 1970s. More than 10 years later we could see where and to what extent there had been an increase. There was none in Sweden, as far as I can remember. The very fact that you have, as in France today, about 60% of the age cohort in the upper grade in the *lycée*, as compared to 6% in 1950, lowers the average. So we are talking about two aspects of achievements nowadays. First, the average level, which by necessity has gone down. Second, you have the spread between schools and students, but particularly between schools. The latter is much higher in countries such as the United States and Britain than it is in Scandinavia. Norway has a very low spread. This is by and large, I think, what one can say about the achievement level and the spread, and how they have been affected by the changes that have occurred.

We showed in the first IEA studies that the top 5% to 10% of the students were at about the same level in most of the industrialized countries. This was an argument in favor of the comprehensive system. The elite tended to be on the same level irrespective of whether you had only 20% or 80% of the cohort in secondary school.

What about the development of quality in education after the comprehensive school reforms?

There is without a doubt a dilemma here, depending on how you define quality, of course. Equality means that everybody gets an equal opportunity. But quality can be defined in so many ways. Are you talking about average quality or are you talking about the quality of the elite?

I try to imagine what is thought of as quality in the general debate now going on. My impression is that most people think in terms of academic achievement. To what degree do you see a contradiction between equality and quality in education?

The person with whom I have discussed this quite a lot is my friend Benjamin Bloom in Chicago. You are certainly familiar with his mastery learning idea. He gave a very provocative lecture about this at the IEA meeting in 1971. He didn't believe in the model distribution for achievement, the bell curve. His idea was that the great majority could be brought up to a high level of excellence by just taking enough time and putting in enough resources.

How do you assess education development in East Asia?

They were very successful there in bringing the majority up to the 80th percentile, instead of having an average around the 50th. I have mentioned Harold Stevenson; he worked with a Japanese colleague, with whom I have been in contact over many years, Hiroshi Azuma, professor of educational psychology. They conducted studies together when I got in touch with them about 25 years ago. Then I resumed the contact when the Nakasone Commission worked in Japan in the early 1980s. The Japanese attitude toward education is part of their culture. For a Westerner, it may look quite confusing. The interesting point is their faith in efforts to achieve. In an empirical study they asked parents in the United States, Japan, and mainland China: "What do you think makes some children succeed better than others, say in mathematics and science?" In America, in spite of the American "creed," they replied that some children were born with better ability. In

Japan and China, they replied: "They work harder, they work harder." This is an interesting basic cultural difference between the United States and the Asian countries.

Speaking of working harder, with very ingenious methods they found out to what extent the pupils worked with the tasks they were supposed to, or how much "time on task." They found that in American schools the time was wasted on all kinds of irrelevant activities surrounding the teaching/learning process in the classroom. The amount of time wasted on irrelevant issues was found to be three to four times as frequent in the United States as it was in China and Japan.

Economics of Education

Economy and education have occupied your research a lot. What sort of events catalyzed this trend in your research?

In the late 1950s we held a Nordic conference in Sweden on the economics of education. A Swedish economist, Ingvar Svennilson, had introduced the thinking on investment in human capital in Sweden. So this was my introduction to this topic. I don't know in what respect I have contributed to it. In 1959 I was invited by the University of Chicago to spend the autumn term there, until Christmas, at the Comparative Education Center. On that occasion I was working with Arnold Anderson. I was introduced to Theodore Schultz, the president of the American Economic Association, who was in the process of writing his presidential address on investment in human capital. Arnold Anderson's wife, Jean Bowman, brought me in touch with Schultz. He invited me to the Faculty Club a couple of times where he tried out his thinking on me. He knew that I had a great interest in the "reserve" of ability. So I became familiar with the kind of thinking on education as a matter of investing in the future, which later on was very useful for me. As a member of the Royal Swedish Academy of Science, I was involved when Schultz got the Nobel Prize in 1979.

To what degree has your interest in the economics of education resulted in your being categorized as an economic rationalist?

I think this is to overstate it. I was not particularly rationalistic or pragmatic about education as a means of investing in either individual or national prosperity. I was simply impressed by the way that Schultz and others, including Ingvar Svennilson, were pointing at the role of education in generating collective benefits, in addition to providing individual benefits. I would say that I was, in a way, strongly impressed by the kind of rationalism that many economists were emphasizing.

Did you see any sort of contradiction to humanism?

No. I think these two things could be married to each other.

You were perhaps emphasizing the pragmatic aspect?

A marriage between pragmatism and humanism, if you wish. A few years after I left Chicago, I became acquainted with Gary Becker, who wrote *Human Capital* in 1964. I met him and other economists many times. After I became a member of the United States National Academy of Education, which met once a year, I made a point of attending the annual meeting. In this way I could be in touch with leading American academics in education.

Could you elaborate a bit on the influence from economics on quality in education?

It had strong impact. One very important event was the OECD meeting in Washington, D.C., in early 1961, hosted by the U.S. federal government. The one who organized it was Philip Coombs. He was then Assistant Secretary of Foreign Affairs and Cultural Relations and was an economist by training. At that occasion, important background papers for the conference were produced by Ingvar Svennilson from Sweden; Lionel Elvin, who was then head of the London Institution of Education; and Friedrich Edding, a German. He was originally a statistician but was interested in the economics of education and particularly education as an investment factor. These three wrote a background paper for the education policy of all the OECD countries at that time — I forget how many were represented, at least 15 or 16. And that was the beginning of my own active involvement in international education policy issues. I had the opportunity of being updated because I participated in most of the OECD meetings that took place on education matters in the 1960s. From these meetings followed a strong drive on the part of the OECD secretariat to promote education as a means of enhancing economic growth.

Were these authors the key intellectuals in the economics of education at that time?

Their papers set the stage, so to speak. It is interesting that this was in 1961, the same year that Ted Schultz gave his historic presidential address at the annual meeting of the American Economic Association on investment in human capital. And this also was at the time when people began to become aware of the role education plays in the competitive edge of nations in the world market. But it was also a few years after Sputnik, where one began wrongly to think that the Russians' success with Sputnik was an indication of their superiority, not only in technology but also in science education. There was a rapidly growing awareness among policymakers, not least under the influence of the OECD secretariat in Paris, that education was a means of competing internationally.

Would it be fair to say that Sputnik symbolized a watershed in viewing education in economic terms?

Yes. It was in the fall of 1957 that Sputnik went into orbit, and it had an enormous impact on American public opinion. The federal government shall not, according to the American Constitution, support formal education. But there are certain exceptions, such as vocational education and national defense. They were trying to find a way of channeling federal dollars into the American system of education because Sputnik was seen as an indication, as I said, not only of Soviet technological superiority, but also of superiority in mathematics and science education.

Before 1957 it was almost considered high treason to visit the Soviet Union. This now became the highest fashion, and they began sending delegations eastward. I met people like George Bereday and Henry Chanecy, who was the head of ETS, and others, breathlessly coming. They didn't even take time to stop over in Scandinavia on their way to or from the Soviet Union. One delegation after the other went to find out about the Soviet system of education and how well they were doing in teaching science and mathematics. They limited themselves to the big cities. They didn't know that it was rather bad in the rest of the Soviet Union and that there was an enormous gap between the rural and the urban areas. In the rural areas there were five-year primary schools. The nine-, ten-, or eleven-year schools were found only in the big cities, such as Moscow and Leningrad. But it had an effect on American public opinion and on American politics. So, in 1958 the United States Congress passed what was called the National Defense Education Act, which was a false label because, according to the Constitution, national defense was a federal task. Nevertheless, the Eisenhower Administration decided to launch a big education program. What I noticed then was all these summer institutes, where they had teachers in mathematics and science getting refresher courses and whatever. Experts from Europe were called over. One of my colleagues in Stockholm, a professor of mathematics, was invited. The big curriculum projects in physics and chemistry were also revived.

The National Defense Education Act provided an enormous increase of funds for, among others, the National Science Foundation, an institution I have followed since it was established in 1950. I became acquainted with John Wilson, who later became president of the University of Chicago, in the late 1940s when he had just taken his Ph.D. and came to an agency called the Office of Naval Research and later to the foundation. The National Science Foundation from the outset had a modest amount of money, but eight years later, in 1958, when the National Defense Education Act passed, they got an enormous increase, and that went on. When I visited them in 1961, they seemed to have difficulties in getting rid of all the money they had been given.

In the landscape around 1960 you had the Sputnik and the awareness of the importance of technology and science for the competitive edge of both the military and economic power of a country. And you had economists looking into education as an investment in human capital. All these circumstances together were instrumental in bringing about the establishment of comparative education as a new field of study.

You mentioned earlier that the American researchers flocking to the Soviet Union after Sputnik did not go for very profound observations. Do you think this superficiality had any consequences later?

What struck me was the lack of interest in the whole country and its education system. An expert on the Soviet Union came out with a book in the early 1960s and was pointing out the enormous spread in education provisions between rural and urban areas. After all, the Soviet Union was still much more of an agricultural than an industrial country. What the experts were expected to bring back to the United States was the conviction that the schools were generally good in the Soviet Union, that they were teaching very well and getting good results.

Could it be part of the misunderstanding that what they found were in fact elitist schools far away from the American ideology of democracy and equal schooling for everybody?

I visited schools in the U.S.S.R. several times, but mostly I saw, as everybody else, institutions in the big cities, Moscow and Leningrad. They were schools where the teaching was in a foreign language. I don't know if you ever met or heard about Tangiane. He was Assistant Director General of UNESCO during the 1970s. He spoke wonderful French. I was able to find out that he had gone to school in the Soviet Union. Well, the teaching from grade one on was in French.

In the 1960s the IIEP (UNESCO International Institute for Educational Planning) organized a visit to the Soviet Union.

When we came to the school, we asked the principal: "What kind of students do you have here?" "Well, this is just a representative group of students, they are from all walks of life." So, I asked the pupils individually: "What is your father?" "He is in the Politburo." It was so evident that this school was for the political and economic elite in the Soviet Union.

Would it be fair to assume that part of the explanation of the success in the Soviet Union's training of experts was that they had an elitist orientation to quality education and a broad and more efficient recruitment of talent than the Americans?

I would be surprised if they actually had been able to broaden the recruitment in the Soviet Union. I cannot tell you, because I didn't become too familiar with the details of how the system operated. In the United States, on the other hand, social mobility through education was on the whole more prevalent than it was in Europe in general. But I would be surprised if they had been able to achieve this in the Soviet Union.

The IEA Studies

We have talked about economics of education and its relation to the Sputnik incident. I would like to move on to the IEA studies, which occupy such a central position in your career. Could you elaborate a little bit on the relation between the IEA studies and what you just have talked about? Is there an obvious connection?

IEA was part of the general pattern. The following happened. In 1952 UNESCO founded an institute of education in Hamburg, with a Norwegian as director, a Mr. Langeland. I was attending a meeting there in 1955. Langeland had the idea of making the institute a meeting place where leading researchers on education could come together and exchange experiences. He also associated himself with William Wall in UNESCO. Wall was a very dynamic person, so efficient that other people sometimes felt offended. He had taken his Ph.D. in educational psychology in Britain. Then he came to UNESCO and was instrumental in promoting international exchange in education research. I learned to know him because I became a member of a committee set up by UNESCO with the task to work out international guidelines for curriculum development both at the primary and the secondary level.

It was in 1955 when we first began that UNESCO work. At the same time, meetings were held for one week once a year in Hamburg. The first dealt with school failure: grade repetition and dropouts, wastage in general. Another meeting was on the use of testing instruments. At the third meeting, which was in a way historical, we dealt with evaluation programs in education, which was a completely new field. The term *evaluation* was not even used in international literature at that time. Willard Olson, who came from a Swedish emigrant family in the United States, then dean at the University of Michigan, came there. We had Wrightstone, the director of research at the City School Board in New York City, who had just written a book about evaluation in schools. At the 1957 meeting we discussed methods of evaluation and how to develop instruments to measure to what extent education goals are achieved. Then in 1958 we had a meeting on comparative studies. At that meeting it was suggested by Arnold Anderson and Arthur Wellesly Foshay that we should try to make a pilot cross-national evaluation study.

We had a second meeting the same year, at Eltham Palace outside London, and it was then decided that we should go ahead with the pilot study. In 1959 the study began.

Who was in charge of that exploratory study?

Nobody was in charge formally, but it was chaired by Foshay under the auspices of the UNESCO Institute in Hamburg. At that time they had a new director, Saul Robinsohn from Israel, who was the director until 1963.

This was a two-year pilot study (1959-61), comprising 1,000 13-year-olds in each of the 12 countries. The purpose of the exploratory study was to find out if it was possible to construct instruments that could be used uniformly in quite different types of countries, all the way from Japan to Sweden, and whether it was possible to

A smiling Torsten Husén dances with an unidentified partner at the concluding banquet of the International Congress of Applied Psychology in London in 1955.

In 1956 Husén was appointed to head the Institute of Educational Research in the newly established School of Education in Stockholm.

Husén (third from right) poses with colleagues on the UNESCO Advisory Committee on Curriculum outside the agency's headquarters in 1959.

collect data which could be processed uniformly. The ones in charge of processing the data were Bob Thorndike at Teachers College Columbia University and Douglas Pidgeon at the National Foundation for Educational Research in the United Kingdom. In the meantime, Bill Wall recently had become director there. In 1961 we held a meeting where the results were available, and we had a preliminary manuscript of the book-size report. We had then tested items in mathematics, science, geography, and reading. We also had included so-called "culture-free" test items, nonverbal ones. The interesting thing, by the way, was that the biggest national differences were found in the culture-free items. Very well translated reading items showed rather small cross-national differences. We also correlated countries in terms of rank order and analyzed the correlation matrix in order to find out whether there were any groups of countries which were similar. We were so encouraged by the outcomes of the study that we decided to go ahead with a main study using fully representative national samples.

And who was now participating in this research group?

All of us were in a way directors or chairmen of research institutions. I was the director of the Institute of Education at the Teacher Training College in Stockholm (*Lärarhögskolan*). We had been established with rather good resources for research on the Swedish school reform. Bill Wall headed the National Science Foundation, and Bob Thorndike headed the Department of Educational Measurement and Assessment at Teachers College Columbia University. Twelve countries were represented. To be exact, there were twelve cooperating research institutes, most of them leading national entities in their respective countries.

Which countries were involved?

Eight European and four non-European countries were involved. All of them were industrialized. The European countries were Sweden, the Federal Republic of Germany, France, England, the Netherlands, Belgium; I think Yugoslavia was also part of it, and the eighth was Poland. Then the four non-European were Japan, Australia, New Zealand, and the United States.

In 1961 we decided at our meeting to go ahead with a full-fledged study in mathematics. The study in mathematics included the same countries as the pilot study with the exception of Yugoslavia and Poland. Instead, Finland and Israel joined.

Why mathematics?

Mathematics was the easiest because of its international language. We decided to constitute an international association of research institutes, the International Association for Evaluation of Educational Achievements (IEA). Furthermore, we established the administration, a chairman and a full-time coordinator, who could be placed at the UNESCO Institute in Hamburg. We hired a young man from Britain, Cobb. This was in 1961. Then, for reasons I will not go into here, there was a kind of crisis. Bill Wall, who had been elected as IEA chairman, resigned. It so happened that I came to the meeting a half-day or a day later than the rest of the participants. When I arrived, they said that a new chairman was needed.

And they had already decided to elect you?

They had already decided to talk to me. So it happened in 1962, when we had just started the mathematics project, that I became the chairman of IEA. We had decided in 1961 to submit a proposal to the U.S. Office of Education for financial support. At that time, they had a total of only six million dollars a year for research. By 1965 this figure had grown to 150 million. We applied for $400,000 or $500,000. First the referees turned us down. But when we were still in Hamburg for a meeting in 1962, we got a message from Washington, D.C., that we had received the grant, which in today's money would have amounted to several million.

How much did you get?

Somewhere between $400,000 and $500,000. It would cover the international costs. It is important to point out that all the costs incurred for the project within the respective countries had to be covered by funds from the country. But in our case we got, as I mentioned, money for the international costs. It was very expensive to bring people together, and the international data processing, which took place in New York at Teachers College, was rather expensive.

Was it easy for the participating countries to raise the money locally?

No, but somehow they were able to manage it. And we had committees working. One dealt with curriculum. This was something we had never done before. We established a kind of grid with all the elements of mathematics teaching on one hand so that we could collect and try them out. Items were tried out in each country separately. So we had a committee working on this; and then, of course, we had to translate the items. The data collection took place in 1964, and the data processing started in the fall of 1964 and went on in the spring of 1965. In 1965, representatives from all the participating institutions came together at the University of Chicago. The meeting was hosted by such people as Benjamin Bloom and Arnold Anderson. We stayed at the Center for Continuing Education over a fortnight in the midst of the winter.

How did you organize your work in this extraordinary group of creative individualists?

We conducted seminars. We had advanced various hypotheses that had to be tested. So when we finished the day, one or two of the graduate students who were helping us went to the computer center with instructions about what kind of "runs" to do during the night. Next morning they came back with the outcomes. Dick Wolf, who was Thorndike's successor, was one of the two graduate students. We wrote brief reports on the testing of each of the hypotheses we had made. We even had a hypothesis committee. I did most of the documentation during 1965-66 while I was at the Stanford Center for Advanced Studies in the Behavioral Sciences. Two volumes were edited by the spring of 1966. That two-volume report came out in early 1967, *International Study of Achievement in Mathematics* we called it, with the subtitle *A Comparison of Twelve Countries.*

How was the math study received by the public?

It was front-page news in the *New York Times* because of the bad showing of the American students.

What were the most visible findings?

We had two international press conferences on the report in March 1967, one in London and the other in Chicago. I had just been on a skiing vacation before going to London. The one in Chicago was organized by Benjamin Bloom. As I mentioned, it was front-page news in many papers. We have books with press clippings from all over the world. Getting publicity, perhaps deserved, made us feel that we should go ahead with another study. Already in the fall of 1966 we had had a meeting in Hamburg where we decided to go ahead with the work, later called *The Six Subject Survey*: reading comprehension, literature, English and French as foreign languages, science, and civics.

This was quite a big project?

Yes. It was reported in 1973-76 in nine volumes, one for each subject field, and one describing national systems of education, one on methodology problems, and one summarizing the results.

Were you the editor of all these volumes?

No. I wrote the preface for each of them, but I was not involved in editing. We had one editor responsible for each volume.

Who were the most actively contributing researchers in this phase?

They were all top scholars. John B. Carroll was in charge of the part that dealt with the teaching of French. Robert Thorndike edited the book on reading comprehension, and the book on science was edited by John Keeves from Australia and by L. C. Comber. The latter was Her Majesty's Chief Inspector of Science in Britain. We had David Walker, who headed the Scottish Council for Education Research. He spent a year with us in Stockholm, and we had people like Lee Cronbach from Stanford. James Coleman, who also visited us, was criticizing, advising, and sometimes documenting things.

I haven't mentioned that the *Six Subject Survey* project was so big that it could not be accommodated in Hamburg. I persuaded the Ministry of Education in Stockholm to provide resources for accommodation at the Wenner-Gren Center in Stockholm. We got nine rooms in the center, a whole floor. The Swedish government also provided data-processing money from the Central Bureau of Statistics. The Bank of Sweden's Jubilee Fund (Riksbankens Jubileumsfond) provided quite a lot of money. The Social Science Research Council gave their share, and then the rest of the money, a considerable part of it, came from the United States. But we were not dependent on the Americans. Currently, the Americans provide too much of the resources for IEA, and they also want to have influence, which is not wise in this type of research, where national pride is at stake.

Who was the minister of education in Sweden during this undertaking?

It was Olof Palme. He was minister from 1966 to 1969. He became prime minister in 1969. He was then followed by Lena Hjelm Wallén as minister of education. IEA had very good support from the Ministry of Education.

Is the Swedish government still supportive?

I have tried to build good relations over the years. I was helping with research in connection with the Swedish school reform.
Also the Volkswagen Foundation in Germany supported us. And
the Leverhulme Trust in Britain. So IEA was multi-nationally
financed. We published nine volumes from *The Six Subject Survey* reporting the international aspects of the project, but then in
each country there were national reports, usually in monograph
form. In all there was a library of some seven meters length that
came out of this effort. We published the first set of reports in
1973. We had an international press conference in Stockholm,
which produced quite a lot of international publicity.

*What about the significance of IEA in the comparative education
field? This big project must have given strong impetus to the
whole field of comparative education?*

The problem that we had with many colleagues in comparative
education was that so many of them had their background in philosophy and history of education and that they were suspicious
about standardized achievement tests for comparative purposes.
For instance, George Bereday, who specialized in the history of
education, said to me: "My friend, you are trying to compare the
incomparable!"

But IEA, of course, had an enormous effect, particularly in
education policy. I have written about this. When I was at Stanford in early 1966, Harold Howe was the U.S. Commissioner of
Education, which was in practice a minister of education. He
invited me to come to Washington, D.C., to brief him about the
outcome of the math study. This gives you an idea of how IEA
was thought of by policymakers. In the Federal Republic of
Germany, they found that in Bavaria, where they had the older,
more conservative system of education, children performed better than in Hesse, where a social democratic reform of education
made it comprehensive. You can imagine the debate that followed
the publication of that finding. In Britain they used the IEA
approach in evaluating the new curriculum in science. And I used

the IEA instruments when I was planning education in Botswana. I found, for instance, that after seven years of primary schooling the pupils in Botswana perform in English at the level of second grade in Britain. It should be noted that, though English was not their mother tongue, it was the medium of instruction.

But there were also problems. In Poland in 1969 somebody whispered into the ear of the Polish minister of education that the data processing would take place in the United States. This raised questions about what the CIA was going to do with the Polish data. I was asked by Polish colleagues, who knew that I would attend a meeting in Warsaw, to go and see the minister. So Wellesly Foshay, Douglas Pidgeon, and I went to see him. When we came into his office — this was about 10 a.m. — the secretary came in and poured what we thought was some kind of fruit juice in big glasses. It turned out to be very strong Russian brandy. So we woke up. After less than one hour, when we had the second glass of this stuff, the minister said, "Oh well, there's no problem, no problem. I will release the data from Poland." But he must have sobered up in the afternoon because we later got the message that the data were not to be released.

Was it at this time you met with Haile Selassie?

Yes, this is one of the particular events from that time which I will never forget. Involved were Jim Perkins, Clark Kerr, and Herman Wells, also a university president. In 1971 we spent a couple of weeks in Ethiopia, primarily to visit and study at the Haile Selassie University in Addis Ababa. We also looked at some other institutions in Ethiopia. Included in our agenda was an oral report to the emperor. We met with Haile Selassie in the imperial palace; he was literally sitting on the throne. We were served champagne. It was a rather pleasant meeting. I even have a photo from the meeting, showing my wife greeting the Emperor. Later I became acquainted with Aklilu Habte, who was president of the university. He continued in this position until the middle of the 1970s and the revolution. Aklilu gained an international reputation. At the UNESCO General Conference in Paris in 1974 he was elected chairperson for the section on education. He was later appointed to the board of IIEP, where I was the chairperson. I was instrumental in his appointment. During a board meeting in Dakar he told me that he was going to return to Addis Ababa. He added that in his absence there had been a revolution, "so they will either execute me or make me a minister." The latter option was what happened. He became minister of culture and sport. However, he did not feel comfortable in this position. My impression was that he did not get along well with the more or less barbaric officers who had seized power. He got an offer from the World Bank and went there to become head of its education department. This department has since been abolished. After the World Bank he went to UNICEF and stayed there until retirement.

Moving back to IEA, how do you assess its significance as a research project up to 1971?

Benjamin Bloom and several others and I were keen to emphasize that we didn't want IEA to become an "international horse race" or Olympic Games. The overriding purpose of the IEA studies was to explain or account for differences between countries in terms of socioeconomic background, school resources, and matters of teaching or instruction, including the curriculum. In the mathematics studies in the 1960s you'll find that the hypotheses we tested all relate to one of the following categories: home background, general socioeconomic background, school resources, methods of instruction, and curriculum provisions. There were repetitions of both mathematics and sciences studies in the 1970s and early 1980s, which I think was important in order to give a longitudinal aspect, but not longitudinal in the sense of the same students being followed up. This gave opportunities to assess student competencies at regular intervals. The overriding objective of IEA was research. We were trying to account for what made education tick.

When you think about your design, methods, etc., are you mainly happy with them? Or are there things you would have done differently if you were to repeat the study?

Given time and the kind of people participating, our approach was rather orthodox in the sense of being psychometrically oriented. We measured; we wanted to quantify. A typical example: We found that Japanese children were performing better than American children at the age of 13. We could show this by looking at mean scores. It was very difficult to account for it in terms of resources because they were smaller in Japan, but we could account for some of it in terms of parental commitment to the school. We asked the children to what extent their parents were asking them how well they performed in school. But this has to be supplemented by going into the classroom and making observations of the kind that Harold Stevenson and his people had done in classrooms in China, Taiwan, Japan, and the United States. But they didn't have representative samples of classrooms. I don't know to what extent this has affected the outcomes, but they have at least been able to look at the cultural pattern and how this is reflected in what happens in the classrooms. On the other hand, to make observations requires an enormous competence among the researchers, not least linguistic competence. So we couldn't include such methods, even though we regarded our approach as somewhat deficient. We had to use as a substitute questions both to parents and students about the kind of motivational factors that might have been influential. No doubt cultural background has an enormous influence if you want to account for the differences between what comes out of school education in the United States as compared, for instance, to China.

Have you noticed recent research that seems to be inspired by the IEA?

Cross-national studies have occurred in several countries — however, not with the same strict comparability that we had. A very prominent strength in the IEA studies was that we were able to use rather sophisticated methods of sampling. We can be sure that within a certain margin of error, we have representative samples of students from the different countries. We had to put in a great effort to make the instruments equally fair or unfair to all the countries. But the Educational Testing Service (ETS) at Princeton did a good job in conducting cross-national achievement studies. There was also an attempt to launch an East European survey. I don't know how far they proceeded in the 1970s and 1980s, or whether they actually conducted any survey. I haven't seen any publications. In that respect, IEA also has had an influence upon national assessments that have been conducted in several countries, such as Britain and the United States, particularly Britain. However, I would have liked IEA to widen its perspective and also to introduce more observational techniques or, on the whole, more qualitative methods, for instance, interviews and classroom observations.

How would you sum up the influence of IEA on comparative and international education?

What we have done in the IEA studies is strengthen the empirical dimension of comparative and international education. The field was dominated by people in philosophy and history of education who seldom made quantitative comparisons, except for using some statistics from administration. There is no doubt that the IEA studies emerged in a situation where there were many factors working together to create a new kind of assessment: cross-national assessments of achievements.

What do you think about the attempts by Eckstein and Noah and others at making comparative education "scientific"?

The first handbook was by Bereday and the other one by Eckstein and Noah. They were pioneers trying to establish the methodology of the field of comparative education by writing handbooks.

How would the IEA approach fit into their ambitions?

Harold Noah was also part of the IEA. He was one of the authors of the nine volumes that came out in *The Six Subject Survey* and was therefore directly involved.

Roots of Adult Education, Education Research, and Student Rebellion

My next queries are about adult education and lifelong learning. Were you involved in this field long before 1971?

By coincidence. When I became professor at Stockholm University, the rector needed to appoint somebody from the faculty to become chairman and inspector of the Adult Education Department. This "extramural" department was not a formal part of the university. But the university was involved because it was affiliated with the university. Thus in 1953 I became chairman of the governing board of the Adult Education Department, and my role also was called inspector. They needed to have a person authorized by the rector to supervise the running of the department. I did this for 20 years, until 1973.

So this was all a Swedish context?

It was a Swedish context, but it was important. When all the Swedish study associations (*studieförbund*) heard that this professor had agreed to serve in the particular role mentioned, they came to me and suggested that I should establish an adult education seminar at the university. This was in the fall of 1953. The participants were leading people in the various study organizations: the workers' movements, religious movements, and the anti-alcohol movement. We had one seminar session per week at the beginning, then we changed to every second week. We focused on problems of adult education, and I published a book called *Adult Learning (Vuxna Lär)*, which came out in 1958 and was translated into several languages. That book has played an enormous role in Sweden. It was used as a kind of guide for people involved in adult education, where a particular type of adult didactics is called for.

You edited this book?

Yes, I was the main editor of the book. I also wrote the first third of it. This book had a second edition in the 1960s. I began to think further about the role of the school as related to adult education. Already in 1960, in a memorandum to the Royal Commission of Schools, I proposed that in organizing a new curriculum for the comprehensive school there ought to be emphasis on basic skills and knowledge that would be needed in order to learn for the rest of one's life. So this was the beginning of the thinking about what in the UNESCO language was "permanent education." *Lifelong education* as an expression came a little bit later. I discovered when I looked into my bibliography that I had written a preface to a journal that began to come out in 1982, the *International Journal in Life-Long Education.* This was before it became a slogan. It was referred to as permanent or continuing education when I first met with adult educators in the United States. I may have picked up more than I realized when I was there in 1954, visiting the Center for Continuing Education at the Michigan State College in East Lansing. It was the Kellogg Lansing Foundation that financed three such centers. At each of these centers you had meeting rooms, restaurants, and possibilities of accommodating people, a kind of small hotel. The idea was that professionals who had a university education and needed to be updated in their competence could come for a few days or for a week or two. You had experts available on campus instead of bringing them in from somewhere else. There was one center in Michigan and another one at the University of Chicago. This idea was picked up by UNESCO and the Council of Europe. The Council of Europe put quite a lot of emphasis on continuing education. The key phrase was continuing in education. Then the idea turned into permanent education. Now it is lifelong education.

These centers make me think of Ivan Illich and his "learning bars." What did you think about his ideas in Deschooling Society?

I was very intrigued by him. I read an article that he had written in 1968, when I was spending half a year at the University of Hawaii. I met him two years later in New York City, where he was invited to the annual meeting of the American Educational Research Association (AERA) to speak on the role of research in education improvement. He and Paul Goodman were on a panel. Goodman was another leading critic of formal schooling at that time. He came from Teachers College Columbia University. The two were competing with each other in saying nasty things about school education. Finally there was a person in the audience who said: "Doctor Illich, what do you think about education research?" Illich answered by taking the conference program, waving it in the air, and saying: "My dear friends, what could be more pointless than investigating the technicalities of the pointless?" Later in 1973, when Ingrid and I were in New Orleans at a meeting, we decided to go to Cuernavaca in Mexico and visit Ivan at his headquarters. Before leaving the United States I phoned Cuernavaca, and a lady responded to me in German, saying that Mr. Illich was in the United States, but she did not know where. So, we changed our itinerary and went to Stanford in California. Arriving on the weekend, I said to Ingrid that I would very much like for us to go to the university library because they had so many interesting books on display. So we walked in, and whom did we see? Ivan Illich! We had the opportunity to have a good conversation right there. He gave us an inscribed copy of one of his books, I don't remember which one. It was not *Deschooling Society*, which I think came later. He was concerned about the Mexican workers in California. This was the encounter I had with Illich. I was very taken by *Deschooling Society*. Formal schooling is not necessarily the only means for making a population literate.

Do you agree that there is less talk about schooling now than in the 1970s?

In a way, yes. Furthermore, the questions of motivation are put differently. My book, *The School in Question*, came out in 1979, after preliminary versions had been discussed at international seminars organized by the Aspen Institute for Humanistic Studies from 1975 through 1978. I criticized the school as an institution in the modern industrial society in several respects. That book is now translated into 13 languages, including Chinese.

What do you think about the relation between education reform and research after Sputnik?

In 1984 I edited, along with Maurice Kogan, a book called *Educational Research and Policy*. There in the introductory part I tried to put together how research and policymaking in Sweden were related to each other.

Research as an instrument in education reform is something that wasn't heard of before the end of World War II. In 1946 the Swedish School Commission got a big grant from the government to conduct studies on "practical" and "theoretical" intelligence, because this was thought to be important for solving the question of differentiation. John Elmgren in Gothenburg was in charge of the project. Then came the reform of access to higher education, a reform also making research necessary, and where I myself got involved. And then finally came the research that just preceded the comprehensive school reform, which was finally legislated in the Swedish Parliament in 1962.

So, in this sense, from 1955 to the early 1960s I conducted studies that were commissioned by so-called royal commissions. This was noticed abroad because there were no counterparts to this in the rest of Europe at that time. The British minister of education at that time called up Stockholm in order to get copies of Nils-Eric Svensson's thesis because it had been mentioned in the *Times Educational Supplement*. Those who were most strongly influenced by the Swedish example were the Germans. Helmut Becker, who founded the Max Planck Institute for Educational Research in Berlin, came with a delegation to Stockholm. Jürgen Habermas was among others in this delegation. They stayed with us for a week, and we went through the various research projects that had been conducted in connection with the Swedish school reform. This must have been in early 1964. When the different *länder* in Germany began to conduct reforms, they also launched research projects.

Another strong experience I had with this issue was in 1965 at a congress on education research in Cambridge. After the congress I was invited by Anthony Crosland, minister of education in the Labour government, to spend a day or two at the ministry to hold an evening seminar with him. We had a very interesting day together. We went out and had a "wet" meal before the seminar took place in the evening. He had brought together people who were involved in British reform. He was strongly in favor of comprehensive education. However, he was not very successful in that respect, not even in his own party. He appointed a Royal Commission, which had the economist John Vaizey as one of its members. A major issue was the so-called public schools. In 1967, perhaps early 1968, I was invited for a session of questioning by the commission on comprehensive education. It turned out that the report they submitted to the government did not straightforwardly recommend comprehensive schools all over Britain. Several leading Labour Party people sent their children to the exclusive public schools. In one of the sessions, John Vaizey told the commission that his son had been accepted at Eton. He said very honestly that had he on principle denied his son the opportunity to go to Eton, he would also have damaged his son's future career, because going through Eton made him a self-evident candidate for Oxford, and after Oxford he would be able to work for the British establishment.

Research in education conducted with the explicit purposes of facilitating education reforms was something rather new after World War II. There was very little before the end of the 1940s.

And Sweden was first?

In a way Sweden was first. We had a head start with the 1946 School Commission.

Why do you think the Swedish authorities were so interested in having such a considerable amount of school research done?

A mixture of boredom and dismay seems to mark the faces of Torsten Husén (left) and his colleagues at an international conference on "Quality in Education," held in Paris in 1966. Economist Sir Arthur Lewis (center) later received a Nobel Prize for his work on development in the Third World. John Vaizey (right), later Lord Vaizey, also an economist, did pioneering work in the economics of education.

I have at least one explanation. One of the members of the 1946 commission was Alva Myrdal. She was the principal of the Stockholm Institute of Training for Kindergarten Teachers. She and Gunnar Myrdal (her husband) had been in the United States, at Columbia, where Gunnar reported on the "Negro problem" in *An American Dilemma*, published in 1944. Alva and Gunnar were great pioneers of social engineering. I still remember from 1947 when the problem of school differentiation was intensively discussed. How could we find out what would be the most suitable way to organize the various tracks? Alva saw this as a challenge for education psychology, and she put these two words together and coined "psychological educational research." So it was not entirely a political matter. Differentiation was a major research challenge.

In Sweden in the 1940s there was a great belief in social engineering and in what research could do to improve education in general. I had the impression that this also applied to Norway.

Was the development in Norway perhaps a bit delayed because of World War II?

Yes, there was a late start in the rest of Europe, while we could rather soon after the war take advantage of experiences from the United States. People were traveling to the United States. Both Alva and Gunnar Myrdal had been there in the late 1930s. Frank Keppel's father, who was the president of the Carnegie Corporation, which commissioned the *American Dilemma* research, brought the Myrdals to the United States from 1938 to about 1940. They returned to Sweden just before the war, but then they succeeded in escaping to the United States and back again during the war. They wrote a book called *Contact with America* (1943). In that book are two interesting chapters on American education with a very glowing description of what education research can achieve. They had their son in the experimental school at Columbia University, and Alva studied that school. The Myrdals are perhaps the strongest example of the hopes during the 1930s through the 1950s that were attached to the social sciences in general, and to psychology in particular, to improve society.

Which other countries do you think have followed or been inspired by the Swedish model of education reform and related education research?

I don't think anyone was taking Sweden as an example, because these big reforms in Sweden were changing the entire structure of the system and thoroughly changing the curricula. The two decades after the war were not the time for this in many countries. This enormous change in Sweden took place over a 30-year period from 1940 to 1970. There are very few similar examples.

I was impressed in the Soviet Union by their curriculum development. I became acquainted with one of the vice-presidents of the Soviet Academy of Pedagogical Sciences. He told me about how curriculum development and implementation can be done in a centralized, totalitarian country. What they did was to have some experimental schools, where the academy tried out a new curriculum. After having done some experiments, probably mostly in urban areas, they decided to introduce the reform all over the Soviet Union. The reform implied rewriting all the textbooks. To force the republics to stick to the new curriculum, they had the same examinations over all the Soviet Union. An effect of this was that in advance of the final exam, the academy sent out a big set of questions that the teachers had to train the students to solve. And among these thousands of items, maybe 30 were used in the final exam.

Was this also true for East Germany?

Oh yes, very much so. The German Central Pedagogical Institute in Berlin, which I visited several times in the late 1960s, had 600 people sitting in the building where Rudolf Hess had been sitting at the beginning of the war. They prepared curricula for East Germany. In the Federal Republic of Germany each *Land* was autonomous in terms of administration, governance, and curricula. However, in order to make *Abitur* (A-level exam), some harmonization among the *länder* was useful. For this and other purposes they established the Standing Conference of the Ministers of Education from all the *länder*. They came together and tried to coordinate. However, this was a voluntary action. It was not found in the constitution of the Federal Republic.

There seem to be similarities between the social engineering in the U.S.S.R. and in Sweden, though Sweden was a social democracy in the West. What do you think?

There are some common elements — for instance, the naive belief in social engineering that you found in the Soviet Union before the period of cynicism. In Sweden there was consensus between the Social Democrats and the Liberals. The Farmers'

Party (*Bondeförbundet*), or the Center Party as it is called now, was in agreement as well. In 1950 I listened to the plenary debate in Parliament about the bill to introduce a nine-year comprehensive school on an experimental basis. I still remember Tage Erlander, the prime minister, getting up and saying: "When it comes to reforms that go to the heart of Swedish society, I have noticed that we are able to achieve quite a lot of consensus." The only ones who voted against this measure, at least in certain aspects, were from the Conservative Party, and they had only 15% support in the electorate. So 85% of the voters went in the direction of improving the society through social engineering as far as education was concerned. It was by and large a society of consensus in that respect.

So 85% of the Swedish electorate had fairly similar values in terms of preferred education policies?

The Swedish Radio Corporation conducted an opinion poll about the school reform. It turned out that in the Swedish population at large even more than 85% were in favor of the reform and saw advantages in it.

Were the reform trends the same throughout Scandinavia at this time, or did you see any interesting particularities, excluding the effects from the war?

In the period from around 1950 to 1970 I could follow what happened in the Scandinavian arena rather closely because every year we held a meeting of the Nordic Expert Committee for Educational Research. My assessment is definite: Denmark was the most progressive. Denmark had introduced training of school psychologists. It introduced a system where the parents were the majority in local school boards. They had schools outside the public system, and all the political parties were in favor of such diversity, even the Social Democrats.

Do you see the presence of private schools in Scandinavia as a particularly Danish phenomenon?

In a way they were private, but they were not selective. They were free — and free to experiment. After all, Denmark had had Grundtvig. I was frequently in Denmark at that time. My impression was that the Danish Institute of Education played an important role. This independent research institute, financed directly by the Ministry of Education, was the stronghold of progressive ideas. Denmark was, in terms of education policies and practice, the most progressive.

Norway had some very progressive people — this goes back to the 1930s — and several were former political radicals. Norway, of course, had *Forsøksrådet* (The National Institution for Innovation in Education). Finland had a tradition of good teacher education. I visited Jyväskylä, which later became a new university. It was a teacher training institution and then became a kind of teacher training university. There was much openness. Finland has in a way been more open to international ideas in spite of long Russian rule. However, they were rather autonomous, vis-à-vis Russia. Many Finnish academics took their Ph.D.s in France or Germany. I have found Finnish academics who have written one book in French, another in German, and a third in Russian. This kind of international openness has struck me as a particularly Finnish tradition. Sweden was more closed to foreign influences, though strongly influenced by the Central European and German traditions. Then, after World War II, came the influence from America.

In terms of American influence on Swedish education, which specific names in addition to the Myrdals would you think of?

I can mention Ester Hermansson at the teacher training seminar in Gothenburg. She wrote an influential book on American schools in the 1930s. Elsa Köhler from Vienna came to Gothenburg and spent a few years there. She wrote a book on reform pedagogy in Sweden during that time. And by and large, the Swedish teachers in general in the 1930s were rather more open and willing to try new pedagogic ways than today.

What effect do you think the Swedish emigration to America had for American influence on Swedish education?

There were connections. But the Swedes in America tended to be rather conservative. L.L. Thurstone is an example. I was sitting with him one evening in Dalecarlia in 1948. We came to talk about Franklin Roosevelt. I said to him: "Three years have elapsed since Roosevelt died, and I guess you have some distance from him. What do you think he has meant in American history?" He darkened and said: "He was the worst liar history ever has seen, perhaps worse than Hitler." I was shocked because I have met very few others with that attitude. He represented the isolationists in America. They hated the man who brought America into the war.

Why do you think that the Scandinavian immigrants to the United States turned conservative and isolationist?

Depending on what period you are talking about, most people came from rural areas, and with the lower-class background they tended to have a kind of conservative attitude that those who are close to the soil often have.

The influence on education that we had from America was mediated by Swedish-American academics. Already in the 1920s there were those who wrote about progressivist American education.

How did you experience the student rebellion in the 1960s and 1970s?

I experienced it in America in 1965-66, when my whole family was at Stanford. The first real student rebellion took place at Berkeley and had to do with the Vietnam War. In 1967, when we had the famous Williamsburg Conference on world crises in education, there were student demonstrations outside. At the dinner, people were placed at tables of eight, and each table was made as international as possible. I was sitting at the same table as the U.S. President, Lyndon B. Johnson. He complained bitterly about the student demonstrations because, I think, he had been accused of giving wrong information to the public about what was going on in Vietnam.

A few months later I came to the Research and Development Center at the University of Hawaii to serve as a kind of advisor. At the center there was a young assistant professor of Chinese origin. Like a large part of the population in Hawaii, he had Asian background. He got a letter of intent, as it was called by President Hamilton, that he would be given tenure. But the governing board of the university interfered, which was exceptional. It practically never happened in America that a university board involved itself in a promotion. It was up to the president to make such decisions. But the board forced the president to withdraw the letter of intent because the young Chinese was an outspoken Maoist. This was, of course, the best way for the president to antagonize the entire faculty and the students as well. There were demonstrations, mostly by students, and this went on and on. Finally he had to resign.

I could observe this because I was in Honolulu from early January until the beginning of June in 1968. On our way back to Sweden, Ingrid and I stopped over in New York City to visit colleagues and friends at Columbia. The campus was occupied by the students, and we could not get access. We heard when we came back to Europe that the police had moved in and cleared the place. At the same time, I heard that it was even worse in Paris. In such places as Warsaw and other cities in Eastern Europe, riots occurred. We had very little of this in Sweden. The students at the University of Stockholm occupied the student union. But, after all, it was their own building.

You think that was more of a symbolic act?

A symbolic act, yes. We already had a system where the students were, at least marginally, part of the decisionmaking process in terms of such things as curriculum changes. The students were on various academic committees. Student participation in decisionmaking bodies had started rather early. I think the Segerstedt Commission on higher education in the 1950s introduced these changes. However, there were certain disciplines where we had problems. One was sociology. The students came up with an unconditional request to have Engels, Marx, and Mao on the reading lists, which could not be accepted. There also were student problems in education, not at the institute I was heading but at the other Institute of Education. They had "big meetings" every now and then. There also were requests that the examinations should be collective and group-based. I rejected these ideas. I didn't have any problem saying that ignorance doesn't become better by being shared. But all in all, I think we had a rather mild form of student rebellion at Stockholm University.

I have the impression that the student rebellion took a much tougher tack in Denmark and Norway. Do you share this observation?

In Denmark I had the impression that the University in Copenhagen was the only one still rather conservative. They hadn't changed very much in terms of governance and curriculum. This might have been one cause for rebellion. In Denmark they had until rather late very few universities. The University of Copenhagen was the dominating institution, whereas in Sweden, Norway, and Finland quite a few institutions were founded outside the capital city.

Higher Education

How do you think teacher training ought to be organized?

My position on teacher training was simply that it should be given at the university, for two important reasons. First, you can not train one category of teachers at what was previously called seminaries, later Teacher Training College (*Lärarhögskola*), or Advanced Institute of Teacher Training. It doesn't suffice to change the plate on the door. This will not undo the prestige gap between primary school teachers, trained at the seminaries, and secondary school teachers, trained at the universities. The latter had the subject training at the university as the core of their competence and identity. But they got their pedagogical training, their practical training, in the School of Education. The second reason was that I wanted all teachers to be in an academic environment where they could have contact with teaching staff who were conducting research.

I would like to have your views on the university's role in teacher training. This differs throughout the world. Let's take Sweden as a starting point. What is the relation between teacher training and the university in Sweden?

An interesting thing is that teacher training was reformed and restructured at the end of the period when we were trying out the comprehensive school. They began rather late. The first Advanced Institute of Teacher Training that was separate from the university was established in Stockholm in 1956. I was involved in its planning. A few years later the government decided to appoint a commission to review the whole field of teacher training because the 1962 legislation on comprehensive school reform introduced it all over the country. I became a member of that commission, and Sixten Marklund was its secretary. At the beginning of our work I wrote a memorandum in which I spelled out the advantages of having teacher training based at the university. Not only did I want to avoid the parallelism, prestige problems, and background differences between the two categories of teachers, but also I wanted a common frame of reference for the two categories of teachers for the first nine grades. I felt strongly that they should be educated within the same institutional framework.

At that time there were quite a few influential people in the government and in the Central National Board of Education who were critical of the university. They saw it as too conservative. My suspicion was that they wanted to have power over teacher training because, if they left it to the universities, it would have been under academic autonomy, which they hated. Central-level bureaucrats always tend to hate autonomy of other institutions in society.

I failed to convince the other commission members. We compromised and proposed a curriculum committee consisting of people from the university and the teacher training institutions outside the university. But the compromise was not accepted by the government. In 1968 a Commission of Higher Education (U68) was set up, and the central bureaucrats wanted to take control of the university. Their strategy had now changed. They no longer objected to teacher training being part of the university. In several parts of Sweden the *Lärarhögskola* was co-opted into the university. For instance, the Malmø Lärarhögskola became part of the University of Lund, and the same happened in Umeå. In Stockholm the university would have become a monster if they had also included 5,000 teacher training candidates into a system that already had some 30,000 or 40,000 students. There the teacher training college was kept outside the university.

In 1966, when I came back from a year at Stanford, I put together a brochure criticizing the government for the strategies it had chosen in this matter. It was called *What Teacher Training Is About*. My overriding point was that reform of the school system required a reform in teacher training to make it appropriate for the new nine-year unitary school. Recently this has changed because of new reforms. But still there are problems. One is those who see education as a scholarly field, mainly as didactics. Didactics is something that has become rather fashionable in Sweden over the last few years. Those who favor didactics do not care much about competence in school subjects, which make up the content teachers are supposed to convey to the pupils. So there are still tensions within the field of education. I find myself as a professor of education in a strange role of saying there is too much emphasis on didactics and too little on subject matter preparation in teacher training.

You think there is too much emphasis on didactics in teacher training in Sweden?

Yes. This is, of course, a strange stand for a professor of education. I feel very strongly that the intellectual weakness we now have in the system of teacher training is because of the neglect of subject matter preparation in favor of all kinds of "garbage" about teaching processes.

72

How do you explain the extremely strong support of didactics among both central-level administrators and the education lobby in Sweden?

I think it's a kind of anti-intellectualism. But it is also, in my view, because of some kind of misdirected progressivism. We have to educate the pupils in a wide sense. But should we then feed them all kinds of useless knowledge?

I have often heard the statement that everyday knowledge, or the everyday experiences of teachers and students, is as important as subject-matter knowledge. How do you feel about the importance attached to everyday knowledge?

I think we are in a serious situation. The quality of those who are going into teacher training has been going down according to most criteria. We are talking about Sweden now. You must realize that over a period of fifty years, the number of young people of age 14 to 20 who are in full-time schooling has been increasing between 400% to 600%. The number of teachers for pupils at that age level also has increased enormously, and the recruitment of teachers has to compete with the recruitment to other professional fields. I don't know whether I mentioned to you earlier that the number of students at my old University of Lund who now take economics, either business economics or economics in general, is equal to the total number of students at the entire university in 1944. There are now many careers competing with teaching. Another constraint is the social problems that, to a larger extent now than before, moved into the school.

Are you indicating a vicious circle here — more differentiated student background in terms of learning conditions, requiring more professional teachers, with the quality of recruits to teacher training going down because of competition with other more attractive professions?

Yes, all this together has had a negative effect. You also have all kinds of changes taking place in society. I don't know how it is in Norway, but the average size of the school units in Sweden has increased. And there is a heavily increased number of specialists in the schools that we didn't have before. The school has become compartmentalized. In the old days it was the teacher who taught, but he was also taking care of many other problems that had nothing to do with teaching. He or she also was a kind of curator or nurse. But now much of this has become specialized, and the atmosphere is much more impersonal because of the number of people involved. Most important, perhaps, is that teacher training today has to cope with the problem of the lowered quality of applicants.

Returning to the secondary school teacher training that has been going on in Swedish universities since 1907, what is your assessment of the quality and relevance of this training?

When I went to the *gymnasium* in the 1930s, we had a category of teachers called "lectors," lecturers. They had taken a Ph.D. in their respective subject areas. And the fact that you had teachers who had been in close contact with research activities meant quite a lot, not only for the students but also for their colleagues, the adjuncts who had only basic degrees. This was a period when the *gymnasium* served a small elite sector. You cannot have it like that now. But we still have, at least in Sweden, a few teachers who have gone beyond the basic degree and have taken a master's or doctorate in a particular subject field.

Are you saying that the fact that some teachers had high academic degrees positively influenced the teaching climate?

The fact that some teachers had a Ph.D. broadened the horizon at the schools. Also, as I have mentioned, we had external "censors" at the matriculation exam. University professors appointed by the government traveled through the country to supervise the oral exams at the upper secondary schools. They could even take over the oral exams without offending the teachers. Several of these teachers were themselves competent for professorships. But since there was only one professorship at each university, many of those who didn't get a professorial chair went into upper secondary teaching.

How does the relationship between the university and teacher training look in an international and comparative perspective?

I must admit that I am not too familiar with teacher training in other countries, except the United States, where I have been a faculty member at two private universities, Chicago and Teachers College Columbia University, and three state universities: California, Hawaii, and Michigan. Without being able to give you a good international perspective, I do see parallel phenomena. The lower teacher competence in mass secondary education was first noticed in the United States. In 1981 I was twice invited to the National Commission on Excellence, appointed by the Reagan Administration. On one occasion I gave my views on the competence achieved by American students as compared to European students at the upper secondary level. On the second occasion, which took place when the commission met at Stanford, we dealt with the recruitment of teachers in the natural sciences. There I heard something rather shocking: Among those who taught science in high schools in the state of California, only one out of six had taken science as a major for the bachelor degree, which was supposed to prepare them for the subject. And California is by no means a backward state.

I wrote about this in an invited paper for the National Academy of Science in the United States. I rewrote it ten years later, because I then had IEA data as a background. This shocking problem can now be noticed in Europe as well. Those who are good in science at upper secondary and who want to take science at the tertiary level want to become civil engineers. Sweden faces this problem, and I think it is similar in other European countries. Those who take advanced studies in science are not going into teaching.

What do you see as the reasons behind this decline?

In the first place, science is unpopular among students because of bad science teaching already at the primary level. The source of recruitment has "sunk." There are fewer taking the science program at the upper secondary level. We find this in Sweden at the present time. So the faculty of natural sciences at the universities in Sweden and in some other countries, as well as the Institute of Technology, are beginning to have difficulties. In my time those who had the highest marks in mathematics and science went to the Royal Institute of Technology in Stockholm and became civil engineers. The universities at that time didn't have any difficulties getting good students for the various departments of science. But this is no longer the case. Our society needs more technicians, engineers, and people who are competent in science, but now it often has to be satisfied with the second rate. The combined effects of bad teaching and lack of interest in science subjects are multiplying, and these factors reinforce each other. Within the next 10 years we are going to have big problems in replacing retiring science teachers.

Is it fair to see this as an unexpected effect of the massification of higher education? Democratization of access has been paid by lowering quality?

In a way it is a price of the massification, especially in countries where there is an almost puritanical equality philosophy. Let's compare the Scandinavian countries with the United States. In the United States one is not afraid of getting an elite. The elite is needed for two reasons. First of all, you have an academic market. You have places like Stanford or Berkeley, who take those students who belong to the top five percentiles. They also recruit from Asia and other countries. In the state colleges or community colleges you find the rest. Everyone with a high school diploma has the right to tertiary education. Clark Kerr organized this system some 35 years ago in the state of California. The top group was admitted to one of the University of California campuses, the next level got into the state colleges, now called state universities, and the lowest level, the two-year community colleges, was for the majority of students. If the student did well at the community college level, he or she could be admitted to the four-year college for the second year. If you did well there, you could be promoted to one of the universities. The Americans kept the tracks open for those who were able and willing to work hard.

How would you pinpoint the difference between the United States and Scandinavia?

We have the same kind of rules of admission. The framework is legislated, and the details are then regulated centrally by governmental instructions of various kinds.

How do Germany, France and England differ in this regard from Scandinavia?

Making the secondary level comprehensive occurred much later on the continent than it did in Scandinavia. In the first and even in the second IEA survey, which was conducted more than 25 years ago, only 9% of an age cohort in the Federal Republic of Germany took the *Abitur*, the matriculation degree, which was the entrance ticket to the university. In France a few more percent passed the *baccalaureat* and took the advanced certificates of education, similar to the A-level in Britain. The introduction of the comprehensive school in Britain increased the percentage. In France there was a liberal policy during Miterrand's presidency, about 1980. Jacques Delors was at that time minister of finance, but he was minister of education for some time. At that time the French decided to increase the number of students in the *lycée* to 60% of the age cohort, and by and large they have done so. In my opinion, they have been more successful than we have. The over-democratized Swedes neglected differentiation. In France you do not request everybody in the *lycée* to take high-level mathematics courses. You offer alternative tracks.

Within the lycée?

Within the *lycée* there are alternative tracks. On behalf of OECD I looked at the French education system in 1969-70. I cannot claim

77

to have followed it in detail since then. But by 1970 I knew quite a lot about it. Having pointed to some dysfunctions of the over-democratized development in Scandinavia, I would also like to point to the fact that central Europe is lagging behind Scandinavia in terms of making upper secondary and tertiary education available.

In Africa I recently heard the slogan: University education for all. What is your reaction to such a claim?

I can understand the claim for "lifelong education for all," even though developing countries first have to solve the problem of providing universal primary education. We have to start with primary education for all, then we can move to the upper levels. We began in Europe to talk about lifelong education or even some kind of tertiary for all in the 1960s, when we had made primary education and lower secondary education available for all.

My query is, however, to which degree do you think it is possible to design university education for all? Or, if that is impossible, are we talking about differentiated tertiary education for all?

It must be differentiated. The university is a place that ought to favor excellence. I mean excellence in teaching and in research, in being at the frontier. Not everybody can be at the frontier. So, it's just like saying that we should have athletics, say "high jump for all." It is an interesting thing, by the way, that if you are talking about the importance of promoting excellence in academic parts of the society, it is sometimes regarded as very suspect and undemocratic, but if you talk about excellence in athletics, then it is all right.

Are excellent researchers at Scandinavian universities feeling guilty for not being equal enough compared to their countrymen?

Maybe in some instances, but more frequently they feel they are perhaps not appreciated according to their quality. I have been a member of the Royal Academy of Sciences in Sweden for many years. The academy is dominated by people in the natural sciences — physicians, chemists, biologists, mathematicians, astronomers, etc. I have the feeling that more frequently they feel they are not properly appreciated than they feel guilty for being excellent.

I would like to continue the topic of higher education, but focus on leadership. What do you see as the most important challenges for leaders of higher education institutions?

I wrote the entry on academic autonomy in the Swedish National Encyclopedia. I have also been involved in the debate that followed when the Report U68 (the 1968 Commission on Higher Education in Sweden) was submitted in 1973. The framework legislation was passed in Parliament in 1975. In this connection, I published the book, *Universities and Research* (*Universiteten och Forskningen*). I criticized the kind of university governance one had in mind. I had become convinced, not only by the Swedish experiences but also by a second OECD review that took place in the Federal Republic of Germany in 1971, about a typical clash between competence and government. I remember a student who said about a person being considered for a professorship that "he is a damned positivist." I mean such expressions expose the problem. I was very strongly against the new system of the universities. The rationale and organization principles were not based on competence.

The overriding principle that has to govern a university is competence. The more competent you are, the more influence you ought to have. Interest groups of various kinds, particularly students, should have a voice but not a vote. This is my view. I saw all kinds of perverse consequences of this business, particularly in Germany, where they for a long time had a very conservative university system. They suddenly had to catch up and remedy all kinds of deficiencies. I think that what they did tipped the balance way to the other side. Have you heard about the *Drittelparität*? The Germans established the principle that one-third of the members of a decisionmaking body should be professors, one-third assistants, and one-third students. But this was sometimes interpreted so that one-third were academic teachers including assistants, one-third students, and one-third other staff, such as secretaries, technical staff, in short, administration people.

In order for a university to be able to fulfill its purposes, it has to promote competence. It cannot be governed by people who have no or very little insight into certain aspects of the activities that are going on. This sounds very conservative, but it is how I see it.

I would like to challenge you more concretely. When you look back, do you recollect examples of excellent leadership of universities?

Oh yes, I do. I have seen and met a number of university presidents. The one whom I admire enormously is Clark Kerr, who happens to be a friend of mine. We have been in touch with each other over the last 30 years or more. I got to know him during the last couple of years of his presidency. He was the one who designed the so-called master plan for the University of California. He was fired by Reagan, when Reagan was governor of California. Reagan gave him the blame for the student uproar. The uproar would have been much worse if Clark Kerr had not been president of the University of California. Another excellent leader was his classmate from Swarthmore College, James Perkins. In the 1960s he was president of Cornell University. Lawrence Cremin, the historian who became president of Teachers College Columbia University, also exercised fantastic leadership. When he accepted the presidency there, he made an agreement with the board that he would have three months off every year, free of all administrative responsibilities. Each year on the first of June he went to the Stanford think tank, where he had an office without a telephone, and worked on his major publication, *American Education*. He was also for some time chairman of the National Academy of Education in the United States.

Did Ralph Tyler hold any leadership position?

Yes, he became the successor of Charles Judd as Dean of the Graduate School of Education at the University of Chicago. Judd had taken his Ph.D. with Wundt in Leipzig. You may have heard about Judd Hall at the University of Chicago. The department is named after Charles Judd. Ralph Tyler became the first dean of the division of social sciences at the University of Chicago until 1954. He then became director of the Center for Advanced Study in the Behavioral Sciences at Stanford, where he stayed until he retired in 1967.

Thinking about American higher education in the 1950s and 1960s, whom would you mention as particularly influential education researchers?

Ralph Tyler is the name that comes to my mind immediately. He was involved everywhere and was very active.

Did he have any party political commitments?

No, but I think he was perhaps closer to the Democrats than to the Republicans. He was affiliated with the Johnson Administration. He was originally trained as a primary school teacher, but I don't know how many years he really taught in school. In the 1960s he initiated a committee that was chaired by John Gardner. That committee prepared the legislation on the research and development centers and funding for education research. It also proposed an enormous program for disadvantaged children.

Then we had James Conant, who was a chemist, but who had much more influence as an educator. As president of Harvard, he appointed a commission after the war, which reported on General Education in a Free Society and which set certain goals for college education in the United States. But Conant also was the man who took the initiative in setting up the Educational Testing Service (ETS). The reason behind this initiative was that Conant realized that one had to take care of the "reserve of ability" in the United States. The system at that time (in the 1940s) was not rational. The United States could not rely just on the quality of people who had been admitted to Harvard, Stanford, Princeton, and Yale because of their parents' wallets. This was not in the long run a satisfying criterion for being eligible for high-quality universities. He wanted a much more rational selection process by simply testing intellectual aptitude.

Having told about Conant and Cremin, whom else should I mention as leaders? Robert Hutchins at Chicago was a fantastic man. He became president of the University of Chicago when he was 29 years old. Before that he was dean at the law school of Yale. I will give you an anecdotal sidelight on him. When I was a student in the 1930s, I read a book by Hutchins, called *Higher Learning in America*. This must have been about 1936. He was born in 1899, so he was 37 years old at that time. But I had the impression that this was written by a man who in a way was extracting the wisdom from a long life in service in higher education. When I came to Chicago in 1959 as a visiting professor, I learned that he had retired in 1951 and had established an institute in Santa Barbara, California. I met him. He had, by the way, received an honorary doctorate from the University of Stockholm in the early 1950s. Anyway, Hutchins wrote quite a lot of interesting things. He was an innovator. He wanted to promote a humanistic general education. He completely renewed, in a conservative humanistic way, the education at the University of Chicago. University education ought to broaden the horizon of the students, and the less pragmatic the better.

Whom else should I mention? Benjamin Bloom, of course. His thinking was much concentrated on mastery learning. I remember a paper he presented, titled *Individual Differences: A Vanishing Point in School Achievement* — individual differences because his idea was that the bell curve is a deceiving device. By means of education you can move the entire curve, or you can press it together to a certain extent.

How do Bloom's ideas relate to Bruner's?

Jerome Bruner had another approach. He concentrated on the teaching process as such and began to renew the thinking about teaching in the early 1960s. We met in Chicago in the early 1980s and exchanged autobiographies. He is a very good writer.

Returning to Benjamin Bloom, you seem to know him well.

He was a most interesting person. His family had escaped from Russia and came to the United States. His father was a tailor. Having come from humble circumstances, he wanted to move up the social ladder. After college he got a scholarship to the University of Chicago in 1938, and he felt a kind of strong commitment to that university. So he is still there. In 1983 Ingrid and I attended a seminar given in his honor when he was 70 years old. Ralph Tyler, his teacher, was there as well. Ben never accepted any administrative positions. They were trying to get him as dean here and there, but he stayed on as a researcher. I believe he made a good decision because I had the impression that he was rather impractical with administrative issues. It was very fortunate for education research that he continued as he did.

What about yourself? You have chaired so many big projects and commissions. Have you ever been tempted or called to be a dean or a president?

I'll tell you how I avoided it. The circumstances were fortunate for me. Back in 1947 when I was 31 years old, the Swedish Employers' Association had an institute that was training supervisors in industry and doing some research. I was offered the leadership of the institute, but since I was so strongly motivated to pursue a university career, I had to say no. The other occasion was in 1965. Ingvar Svennilson, who was then dean of the social science faculty at the University of Stockholm, and Erik Lundberg, an economist and the most senior of the professors on the social science faculty, came to me and said: "We have seriously thought about finding a successor to Ingvar, and we have concluded that you would be best suitable to be the new dean." I said that I felt very flattered about this, but the problem was that I had decided to go to the Stanford think tank for the next academic year, and I could not back off from that decision. So I said: "If you want to have a dean who is on leave during the first years of his office, take me." That was the end of that story.

But I did head a couple of institutes. First was the School of Education, where I had a staff of some 25 to 30. In my administrative positions I tried to delegate all the detail work. I jumped in when it was necessary to see some important people in order to get money or things of that sort.

You have created three research institutions in your life. Are you an entrepreneur?

Not really. But I must admit that I wanted to do something new, even though in certain respects I am very much a slave of habit. I am not very happy about making the major features of my life a routine, which perhaps explains why I have been traveling so much, even at the age of 80.

We keep staying in the 1950s and 1960s. Looking around the world at that time, where did you see excellent research environments or universities?

From 1964 to 1978 I was on the board of the Max Planck Institute in Berlin. Conant, by the way, was also a member but not the whole time. For a short period we even had Pierre Bourdieu on the board. This institute was set up by the Max Planck Society in Germany. It has been able to attract top researchers from around the world. For instance, they recruited Paul Baltes, a German by birth, who held a prestigious professorship in the United States. The Max Planck Institute had a lot of resources and created a very open research environment. But if I look at the other places from which I have concrete experiences, I would say the University of Chicago. In the years after Ralph Tyler, it continued to flourish. When I was there on sabbatical in 1959, one still felt his ideas and presence. Furthermore, he recruited a good successor, Frank Chase. He had creative ideas, such as having joint appointments with other institutions. In this way he got hold of people like Jim Coleman and Jack Getzels, who was also a psychologist. Philip Jackson and others were recruited to Chicago. Another idea he entertained was that there should be an experimental school, which was even in the same building where the students were taught.

This reminds me of Dewey and his Laboratory School. Is there any connection?

Dewey came to the University of Chicago in the 1890s. He was one of the first who was recruited to this new university, which was founded in 1892. Dewey founded the famous Laboratory School in 1896.

Comparative Education Impressions Worldwide

Looking around the world, which countries do you see as the more interesting ones in terms of their education policies?

The United States stands out for two reasons. First, it came up with the melting pot philosophy. Education should be the main instrument of creating a new nation. That's why there was no talking about teaching the mother tongues. People came from all parts of Europe at that time. Initially the blacks were not part of the nation, but later they were. Second is the local initiative. Schools were set up by the local community, not by the states or by legislation passed in the parliament and initiatives by the government. The Constitution says that the federal government has nothing to do with education, and the states could at best give some financial support. There was a state board of education, which set the framework. Beginning with the Puritans in New England, primary schools were set up. The next thing that happened was that they set up high schools. In Europe, the grammar schools or *gymnasia* were set up by the central governments. There was a long centralist tradition in Europe from the Middle Ages. There, the secondary grammar schools were elite schools, while their counterparts in the United States were for almost everybody. Then in the 19th century came the universal primary schools in Europe. In America setting up the primary school was the first stage. When there was a need for secondary education, or further education, they set up what they called the high school, because it was "higher" than the primary school. That is why the *gymnasium* in Europe has no real counterpart in the United States. In the United States, college in a way is something between the university and the European gymnasium. In a nutshell these are the typical features of the U.S. system of education.

Is it fair to speculate that this decentralization of education policies, founded in the U.S. Constitution, could be a straightjacket for federal education policy ambitions? Some years ago President Bush was eagerly talking about the need for a national curriculum. What is your opinion?

I don't think so. I mean, they have already deviated from the provisions of the Constitution by setting up national goals, which the U.S. Congress passed a couple of years ago. These laws imply that some 8% to 9% of the total expenditure for schools comes from the federal government. The federal government may try to influence policy directions by this support. But to really take charge? I cannot see how that would be politically possible.

What about German education?

The Germans finally succeeded in reforming the system, at least partially. It was a very hot political issue. I debated this many times with German colleagues. They had a parallel system of schooling from 10 to 18 years of age, longer than in other countries. So, in certain *länder*, such as Hesse, they had *gesamtschule*, whereas the parallel school system prevailed in other *länder*, where you spent four years in the basic school, and then you transferred to the nine-year *gymnasium*. They also tried a kind of French compromise, a stage in between, called the *förderstufe*, where it was not decided whether you should go on according to the primary school curricula or whether you should be definitively incorporated into the academic secondary school. The system is not as rigid as it was, but there are still traces of the parallel system. The Germans now have a much higher percentage of students going on to academic secondary school than before.

Turning to Japanese education, do you see it as a success or a tragedy?

There are contrasting views on Japanese education. Harold Stevenson and his group have shown that the Japanese students are happier than those in the United States. They asked the same question to representative samples to find out about stress symptoms and the like. There is even more cooperation in Japanese classrooms than in Europe. The Japanese also are affected by Confucian culture. I wouldn't regard myself as a specialist on Japanese education, but I visited Japan in the 1960s and 1970s and spent one week there every year from 1983 on. In the 1980s I was invited to serve as an expert by the Nakasone Commission. The commission was doing an overhaul of the entire education system. In 1983 I spent one week with the commission in Tokyo and another week in Kyoto, and the same happened in the following years. The last visit was in 1991.

Japanese education has to be seen within the framework of the Japanese culture. It cannot be copied. I mentioned earlier the comparisons between Japanese classrooms and the classrooms in Europe or in the United States, which showed that school work is much more goal-directed in Japan, much more concentrated, with more time on task than in, for instance, the United States. Then there is the heavy workload. There are more school days per year, more homework; and they also have these "coaching schools," the *jukus*, which have increased over the years. They provide extra training possibilities for students and parents who wish to catch up with what's going on in the regular school. When President Reagan and Prime Minister Nakasone first met, they each decided to appoint a commission that would take a look at their respective education systems. I recommend strongly the report that the American researchers wrote about Japanese education. They gave very insightful descriptions. The Japanese study of American education was not as good because they were too polite and too uncritical. They did not want to label things by their proper names.

You have indicated the influence of Confucian philosophy in Japan, and the Americans obviously had some effect in their efforts to change Japanese education after World War II. What about other Western influences on Japanese education?

As a matter of fact, the Japanese were for some time extremely systematic. They tried to borrow the best they could find, so about one hundred years ago they sent educators to Europe. They visited and studied French elite institutions (*les grandes écoles*) and tried to copy them in planning the universities of Tokyo and Kyoto. They were much impressed by German bureaucracy in education, and so they took over something from the Germans. When they built their university and the upper secondary systems, but particularly the university system, the idea was to copy the best in the West. In the 1950s the Japanese Ministry of Education set the goal for education planning and implementation in such a way that the country would double its GNP in a decade. They succeeded — ahead of time.

Looking again at your own country, what do you see as lasting successful achievements of the Swedish model of education?

I think it was the establishment of the common nine-year school and the role played by education research in connection with that reform. The main preparation and general planning were made by two committees, following each other in the 1940s. The first one was more of an expert committee, and the second one was more political.

At the beginning the political one was chaired by Tage Erlander, who was in 1945-46 the minister of education and who in the 1930s had headed the editorial office of the Swedish Encyclopedia (*Svensk Uppslagsbok*). He had a very deep veneration for academic achievements, having spent many years in the university city of Lund. During the time he was in charge of the encyclopedia, he met representatives of the various academic fields. When he then became prime minister, he showed a very high appreciation of the role played by scientists or researchers in general in building a new society. He had a background in behavioral sciences as an economist; but he was also trained in the natural sciences, and he had a close relationship to some of the leading natural science researchers at the University of Lund. In 1962 he set up a standing body of advisors, called the Research Advisory Office, to help the government frame research policy in Sweden. I happened to be one of the members of this group. We were about 20 professors. Erlander took a great interest in the discussions of the group. We met for several days a year with him as chairman, discussing research priorities. I still remember in 1964 or 1965 when Ingvar Svennilson, who was one of the three members from the social sciences, proposed doubling the resource allocations to the research councils over a five-year period. This actually occurred from 1963 to 1968. This was while the economy of the country was steadily growing, and these years were very favorable for Swedish education and research. It was a powerful era of social engineering.

Can any other country equal having three ministers of education who later became prime ministers?

No. Sweden is the only one. Erlander was minister of education in Per Albin Hansson's cabinet for one year. When Per Albin Hansson died, Erlander was his successor. In 1969, after 23 years as prime minister, he was succeeded by Olof Palme, who was then minister of education. Palme was succeeded by Ingvar Carlsson as minister of education in 1969.

And even the present prime minister, Göran Persson, served as minister of education. That makes four of them?

He was the minister of schools, not of education. Since the 1970s we have had a system of two ministers in the field of education, one for the whole area of education and science and the other with a responsibility limited to primary and secondary schools.

Turning to the south and looking at countries labeled as developing and their education policies, what comes to your mind as interesting events in the 1950s, 1960s, and 1970s?

What immediately comes to my mind are "the tigers." I was in Singapore in 1971. I think the prime minister was named Lee, a graduate from Oxford with a Chinese background. He was like a strong authoritarian father ruling the country like a family. The fact is, however, that an almost unbelievable development has taken place there in terms of annual increase of GNP. In the same region you also have South Korea and Japan. I think Singapore is the most outstanding example of a developing country becoming very developed. Singapore paid special attention to its education policies.

What about the African countries?

It is not very encouraging to look at Africa now. I read the documents for the meeting of the African ministers of education in Addis Abeba in 1960. UNESCO brought them together, and ambitious resolutions were passed, as usual. I think it was expected that by 1975 illiteracy would be practically eradicated. It was given top priority in planning and budgeting. In Nairobi in 1968 the education ministers again got together. It was found that in absolute numbers there were more illiterates in Africa in 1968 than in 1960. I am talking about absolute numbers. Instead of putting enough money into primary education, it went into tertiary education. A university student in a typical African country costs the public purse a lot, perhaps a hundred times as much as a primary school student. The third meeting took place in Lagos in 1976. All the indicators showed that little improvement had taken place. So you have to ask yourself what has gone wrong in planning and implementation. My own, not too enlightened conception is that they do not have their priorities straight. They have focused too much on secondary and tertiary education. At those levels schooling is very expensive. They also were rather spoiled in the tertiary sector. I remember in Botswana there was a strike among the university students. The students had allowances from the state. The state paid tuition for them, as well as expenses for food and living. Further, the state guaranteed them jobs in the public sector after graduation. What happened was, because of a mistake, those who were hired and got salaries immediately after graduation also got allowances as university students, and so they had both salary and subsidies at the same time. When this was discovered the government required them to pay back at least one of the two. This claim caused a strike.

I saw something similar in Egypt. In 1979 the IIEP held a meeting in Egypt on higher education. There the university students also were guaranteed jobs in the public sector, and there was an enormous overproduction of graduates. Egypt could, however, export quite a lot of their university graduates to the other Arab countries, for example to Saudi Arabia and other rich oil countries on the Arabian peninsula. It would have been an enormous advantage for primary education in Egypt if the cost for training these university students had been transferred to the primary sectors. This has to be viewed together with the conception that I have had on the inadequacy of the European model of formal education for the developing countries. I am not very hopeful as long as most donor countries stick to the idea of just pumping more and more into formal education. If you look at the UNESCO and the UNDP statistics, you will find that for most of the poor developing countries there has been no economic improvement. At best they stay at the same level as some 20 years ago, and in many cases they are going down. Worst of all is that the students in the developing countries were given hope that, within a few decades after the colonial period, everybody would be literate.

If you compare Africa and Latin America, what do you see as the most striking differences?

There are huge differences. In Latin America you still have a kind of a replica of Spain. The indigenous population has, by and large, been wiped out. There are only small numbers of descendants of the original population. With the exception of Brazil, all on the South American continent speak the same language, while in Africa it is dramatically different. Take Botswana as an example. The country tried to make English the standard language of instruction at all levels. My view was that it couldn't work. The National Commission on Education that I chaired suggested that the mother tongue, Setsuana, should be used as far as possible, before switching to English. It was a shocking experience to learn that in countries such as Angola and Mozambique the decision was taken to use Portuguese as the medium of instruction from the first grade on, because they could not find enough support for any of the tribal languages. I used to make the following parallel to a British, Swedish or German audience: Imagine if we would decide in our countries that after grade four Chinese should be the medium of instruction.

Part Two
PRESENT

International Education Trends, 1971-96

With the stage having been set by our discussion of Torsten Husén's early career, we turned our attention to events of the past three decades, roughly the 1970s, 1980s, and 1990s.

Education: Research Field or Academic Discipline?

Some people claim that education is a science. Others disagree. What is your opinion?

I gave my views on that question in an article in *Svenska Dagbladet* (*Swedish Daily*) in March 1996, and it caused some kind of upset. I mean, the matter is very simple; education is a practical activity. It has to do with bringing up children and teaching them in the classroom. This applies also to adults who are trying to add to their competence.

Goals relevant to education are a matter of the philosophy of didactics, and the methods are derived particularly from psychology. Psychology has been the main scientific discipline related to education. Education is a meeting place for various academic disciplines.

This doesn't mean that I deny that education is a field of study and research. It is indeed a field of study at the university. You have to make a difference between a field of study and a discipline. A field of study can be a meeting place for several disciplines. That's very briefly how I see it, and in my book on education psychology, which came out in its first edition in 1957, I quote William James in *Talks to Teachers on Psychology* (1899). This book consists of published lectures that he gave to teachers at Harvard in the 1880s. James started the first lecture by stating that "you make a great mistake if you think of education as a discipline like, for instance, psychology."

Then how do you explain the birth and development of the idea of education as a discipline?

You must keep in mind that education has a reputation as a field of study. I am talking about it as a department or faculty of education, or as a research institute of education. Its reputation often is lower than other subjects, and to a large extent this is simply because it is borrowing from established disciplines. There is another thing I have noticed over the last 25 years. The idea of education as a discipline is attracting people who think they can improve the world and have enormous pretensions to do so. We had this kind of social pedagogical movement in Sweden as well. I will give you an example. In the summer of 1954 when I gave some guest seminars at Teachers College Columbia University, I met with Ralph Spence, who was then dean of graduate studies in education. I sat in his room, which faced 120th Street, and Ralph said to me: "The street you see here is the broadest street in the world. On the other side you have the rest of the Columbia University — the faculties of arts and science. On this side you find education. In academic terms this is Broadway."

This incident also reminded me of my reaction when I heard that there are 1,050 professors of education in Germany and Austria today. In the early 1950s there were perhaps a hundred. It is not that simple. These professors do not necessarily possess the kind of methodological straightness of thinking that has to be required from good academics. The titles are covering shallow competency.

What is your attitude toward qualitative and quantitative approaches?

I felt very strongly about this dichotomy when I was a student because my professor and supervisor of my advanced studies in the field was a humanist and not a natural scientist by background. He was a philosopher and a historian. He had studied with, among others, Riclert and Windelband in Heidelberg. They were skeptical of the quantitative approach as used in psychological testing. So I became aware of this kind of dichotomy. As already mentioned, the IEA studies were, in a way, extremely quantitative. After all, those who were doing this study were leading people in education testing, such as Thorndike and Bloom. We found this to be "firm" knowledge, verified knowledge so to speak, because we found facts by measuring. Sometimes we lacked further information and had to use classroom observations. But even observations can be systematized in a quantitative way, that is, you can count certain kinds of behavior.

When talking about this dichotomy between quantitative and qualitative matters, I think one has to consider what is referred to as "understanding" by Wilhelm Dilthey. It was not called hermeneutics at that time. This is a more modern term. To understand, one has to be a part. It is, in a way, like diving into the process and trying to grasp certain aspects of a phenomenon that you can not grasp by quantitative methods. It is difficult. I have always had problems being precise in indicating the difference between quantitative and qualitative approaches. The problem is, of course, how to prove or verify what you were saying about the outcomes of your study. But I have no dogmatic position here. As I pointed out earlier, I think that if we find the average score in mathematics in Japan is superior to the one in, say Sweden, you can go into the classrooms and begin to observe, you can interview teachers and parents. Then you may come up with certain explanations based on an understanding of what they mean when they say this or that.

I think I see problems in this field between a declared subjectivist approach and an intended objectivist approach. Some people would say that certain phenomena can be understood only by understanding others' understanding. Then you have to interpret. When trying to communicate these interpretations, you have to apply a more or less standardized language, certain concepts, certain generalizations. By doing that you put restrictions on the interpretations. What do you think are the range and limitations of an interpretive, hermeneutic approach?

We are in a difficult situation. In 1989 I wrote an article for the UNESCO journal *Prospect* called "Educational Research at the Crossroads." The point I made there is that classroom phenomena are unique. You have a unique teacher teaching unique children in a unique situation. And the impossible ambition of science is to generalize uniqueness, which in the last analysis means trying to arrive at recipes. This is a central problem. What I am discussing in that article is how teachers get so frustrated by education researchers because they expect education researchers to reveal generally applicable principles, to come up with recipes. The knowledge that they arrive at should be usable not only in a particular situation, but in all the other ones as well.

The consequence of what you are saying now could be that a lot of such research at classroom level is useless except for those people involved there and then.

I am simply saying that I question this type of research as being called scientific. One of the characteristics of scientific research is that it can be generalized from one situation to the other. This is not possible in most of the things we find when we are practicing education. I would also like to make another point, namely that you can do useful education research where you arrive at generalizable outcomes. Let's take the relationship between school performance and social background. You can make a study of, say, 10 schools in Oslo with outcomes applying to the schools in Trondheim. You are getting away from the unique and the individual to the general and universal.

Would such a study tell us what the different motivation in different social groups is?

It could be motivation, it could be all kinds of things, such as the usefulness of having parents who are educated, or whatever.

96

But as soon as you study a group of individuals you arrive at some kind of average. But you cannot generalize from observations in one particular classroom, you have to have many. Let me explain. I noticed when I visited a classroom in Japan how concentrated the students were. I found the same when I visited 20 other schools. So I feel quite convinced that I can generalize and say that students in Japan are different from those in the United States. In the natural sciences you can arrive at generalizations much easier than you can when observing children in the classroom.

Is there some sort of parallel to the different subjects you had in the IEA study? You chose mathematics, which was simpler than languages. Is it possible to see the implications regarding school improvement or pupils in general if the key factor is the quality of teaching? Or can one only hope that classroom instruction will be of quality?

Let me give you an example from the Coleman studies. He called it the educational opportunity study, and it was conducted in the United States in the mid-1960s. He used a big sample of American students. He could convincingly show how much parental background accounted for differences in educational attainment. I'm expressing myself very carefully now. It accounted for more of the variances between *individuals* or between schools than teaching did. After this you were met with a kind of pessimism when you attended conferences in the United States in the 1960s. The question was: Does schooling make any difference?

The point I'm making in the *Prospect* article is that if you want to arrive at didactic recipes or principles, it is much more difficult than arriving at generalizations about the importance of social background or availability of financial resources or whatever. In the latter case you cut through a lot of individual situations, but in the former case you are not in the same favorable situation. You have to be much more comprehensive in covering facts to arrive at something that will give you didactic guidance and recipes.

Curriculum studies are part of the field of education. Are they social science or humanity studies?

I never thought about that. In 1956 in Sweden we launched an enormous curriculum project for which I hired a young assistant, Urban Dahllöf. We worked together for several years, and we delivered background documents pertaining to the curriculum in the comprehensive school in 1960. Urban did similar studies for the *gymnasium* in the early 1960s. My idea was that curriculum studies should be based on empirical approaches. What was needed in terms of adult competence? If you stayed in school at the age of 16, you either went on to the *gymnasium* or to a vocational school. We tried to find out what the *gymnasium* needed as a base competence for its programs and what sort of base they expected from the previous stage. A third option for the students would be to go directly into jobs in industry or business. So we made a very thorough study of those who received the "products" of the nine-year comprehensive system, what they needed and what kind of competence the young people needed in order to fit the jobs. But we did more than that. We also tested people who were already employed in industry and business, people who had been out of school more than ten years, to find what level of competence they had.

What is the role of statistics in education research?

Descriptive statistics is necessary. You need to know how many are enrolling, how many are examined, how many are dropping out, etc. And the authorities need to know how many are born in a given year in order to be able to tell how many will enter the schools. Analytical statistics is, like other mathematical tools, intellectually demanding and therefore controversial. But there is no doubt there are certain things that can be thoroughly elucidated by analytical statistics. Dr. Zhao, a young Chinese colleague in Stockholm, did a multivariate study of the outcomes of science education in Chinese schools. At least a certain minimum understanding of analytical statistics should be required. I was never outstanding in statistics myself, but I tried at least to understand its meaning and to see its importance in the context, not least related to empirical methods. This is the other side of the coin. When you collect empirical data you need to have analytical instruments in order to understand where many factors are influencing a given education phenomenon.

Action research was a buzzword at the university in the 1970s. What is your opinion of it as an academic activity?

I was intrigued by this in 1954. Stephen Corey wrote a book on action research in the late 1940s. He was a professor at Teachers College Columbia University. He coined the phrase. Back in Sweden I used the idea in connection with research on the Swedish school reform because there was a suggestion that certain experimental schools should be established. Instead of the six that had been suggested, we got only one in Linköping. Action research was conducted there.

How might Dewey have contributed to influencing education in the direction of action research?

Dewey may have contributed to action orientation because of the kind of philosophy he represented, his kind of pragmatism. He lived until 1952, if I remember correctly, and he was also at Columbia University. I mean he was in the true sense more philosophically oriented. I think he was blamed without justification for the so-called progressivism in education.

Current Issues in Education

I would like to have your opinion about the changing quality of teachers. How do you react to the following statement: The quality of teachers in Sweden in primary school was higher in your youth than it is today because teachers' status, public attitudes toward teachers, and the motivation among students have changed.

We can simply put together statistics, say, the grade point average of those who went into teacher training in 1920, as compared to 1990. It was much higher then. Also in terms of social mobility, teaching is a much less attractive occupational choice today.

So following your line of thinking, in order to increase teaching quality one would have to increase teacher salaries?

That is one step that has to be taken. But you see there are so many additional factors one has to take into account, for instance, parental commitment. But it is in a way very disappointing to find that from 1960 until now, both in the United States and in most of the European countries, the real cost per year per student, in uninflated money, has become two to three times higher. And if we look at student competence, what do we see? In mathematics, we have now a study from the 1960s and another from the 1990s, and in science one from 1970 and another from 1995, and we find that there is very little increase in student achievement. When I am nasty I say to teachers who claim that they lack the financial resources to improve education: Well, we improved financial resources by 250%, but are the students two and half times as knowledgeable as they were in the 1960s?

Let me challenge you. If you could have all the money you ask for in order to improve the quality of teaching in Sweden's lower secondary school, what would you do to raise the achievement level?

I am afraid I cannot be very specific. One factor that has increased the costs is that the use of the existing personnel has deteriorated. If you look at how many students per teacher we have, there is statistically one teacher per nine students. If you are going to the classroom, you often find more than 20 students. Teachers are apparently spending more time outside the classroom than before. Then you have all kinds of specialists. I was one of the founders of the Swedish Psychological Association in the 1950s. We had 80 members. Can you imagine, they now have 7,000. I don't know how many of these are school psychologists. I am concerned that in spite of increased costs, we have not improved our schools very much. Related to this is the fact that today's social problems have moved into the school.

What do you think about privatization as a means of making schools both more effective and efficient?

We have certain leads in this direction, namely the Coleman study, *Public and Private High Schools.* In the United States about 10% of the students are in private schools. Most of these private schools are Catholic, run by sisters very poorly paid but extremely committed to their work, and they have students whose parents are also committed to schools. The cost per student for these schools is lower than in the public schools. The learning outcomes in these schools are higher, decisively higher than in public schools.

It's true that those who are dogmatic socialists or central federation trade union leaders do not like private schooling. I do not like private schooling either if it reflects the economic means of parents who put their children there. I think Denmark is a good example of a private system where private or independent schools are given opportunities to be innovative and inspire public schools.

What do you see as the main problems of international comparisons of education systems' efficiency?

It depends what kind of comparisons you want to make. If you want to compare enrollments, examination frequencies, dropout rates, or grade repeating, all these phenomena can be compared cross-nationally. There are no difficulties in doing so. However, it can be difficult to say what is meant by enrollment and so on. Over the years the International Bureau of Education, as well as the Council of Europe, collected information from the ministries of education around the world about such things. When it comes to outcomes, to the "productivity" of the systems, one runs into difficulties. That is why the IEA was established.

It was quite evident, at least for us who started this, that we had to construct criteria and instruments for measurement that were internationally valid and applicable. Then we met three problems. First of all, to what extent is a given yardstick adequate for a curriculum in a particular country? Particular elements in the curriculum were in focus. Was the specific element taught at the 13-year-old level, had it been taught before or later? I'm especially thinking of the various topics in algebra, which in some countries are taught already to 12-year-olds and in other countries a couple of years later.

The second problem was the level of difficulty of wording. This problem has to do with translation. In most cases problems have to be presented verbally. We translated the item and then had it independently translated back. We compared the second translation with the original, which then gave us a fairly accurate picture of whether the translation had succeeded. These were important methodological problems we had to manage.

Furthermore, there are problems of definition. I discovered this at a UNESCO conference in Paris in early 1956. We were discussing the collection of information. Take, for instance, the stage called secondary education. What is meant by secondary education in different countries? Secondary education in 1956 in Britain was very precise in the legislation, it was schooling after the age of 11. In Sweden, secondary meant the stage after six or seven years of primary school. In America secondary school was called high school, after either six or eight years of primary school. The United States has two systems, either four or six years of high school. So there are certain difficulties at the conceptual level and, as I said, they are establishing criteria that can't be made comparable internationally.

Thinking about developing countries, is there any alternative model to Western schooling as developed from ancient Greece?

No, not schooling in the systematic way we are conceiving it. But you have the elders who were wise and who shared their wisdom with the young.

Nelson Mandela in his biography actually refers to the chiefs' wisdom and teaching as a form of "local education." How relevant is this in an era of globalization?

That's a point that I have made several times. I talked to René Maheu about it when we had that meeting in Bellagio in 1972. The Western model we have exported is inadequate to the so-called developing countries because it does not fit into their societal or cultural context. I try to show this by referring to our own history in Scandinavia. We seem to take for granted that there are universal models for organizing formal education. You find this, for instance, in the Delors Report. The "bleeding heart liberals" think that the Western model is a universal blessing. To them the solution is just to introduce universal, full-time primary education for at least a half-dozen years in a given country. Then we think we have done something very good. Actually, we may have contributed to destroying the family as a working team. Where the children begin already at the age of five or six to look after the cattle and they are needed back home, they learn quite a lot by working with their parents. This is education of another type than the formal one. Let me be very specific and point to one example in Botswana. We went out one day on an excursion in the Kalahari Desert and came to a village where schooling was taking place. There were so many children that most of them were sitting under trees outside the school house. They were sitting in groups, just as in school, and in one group there was a blackboard. It must have been the last grade of the primary level, and the teacher was coaching them for the final exam, which was issued by the government. The teacher had written questions on the blackboard. I still remember the first question: Who was the first supreme commander of NATO? I said to Peter Williams and the others in the group, "Who the hell in this country cares about who the first supreme commander of NATO was?" There were several questions of this type in the section of the final exam called general knowledge, what the Germans call *Allgemeinbildung*. This raises, of course, questions of relevancy.

Can we extend this reflection to education reforms in our own region? What do you think about the Norwegian and Swedish principle of concentrating so much on having vocational educa-

tion within school buildings, instead of making more use of an apprentice system?

The German apprenticeship system is perhaps the most outstanding feature of modern German education. From the age of 14 to 18 many spend some 10 hours a week at school and the rest in the enterprises. They are given the opportunity to relate the kind of competence they acquire in school to their workplace and vice versa. The main problem is now, as we saw it in the Academia Europea report, that the industrialized countries in Europe have problems in making schooling meaningful. A high percentage of teenagers in Europe and the United States find it completely meaningless to be in school.

What about the role of the parents in influencing students' motivation for schooling?

Usually one leaves out the family in planning education. I already pointed out the importance of children as working partners in the family. This is not a kind of slavery or child labor in the sense of working in a factory. Working with the parents, doing what they are able to do, already at an early age, this is an important aspect of the educational process. That is why we found in Botswana that even after seven years of schooling, there are certain competencies they have not acquired because they are irrelevant. They don't know who the first supreme commander of NATO was.

To UNESCO's ideas a time back, you hinted jokingly of a sort of universal curriculum or universal curriculum guidelines. Is it possible to imagine a small, core, universal curriculum to which every citizen of the world should be exposed?

In very general terms, it is not too difficult to devise a universal core curriculum. It would consist of communication skills, reading, writing, reckoning/arithmetic, and the skills connected with learning how to find and process information.

When you said communication skills, what do you have in mind?

In the first place, the mother tongue, and then, of course, some basic things that have to do with history and geography of the world. I mean very simple things.

Do you think it is fair to claim that part of the development aid from the North to the South has implied cultural imperialism or neo-colonialism?

In a way, of course. Aid is provided in a way that has certain features of neo-colonialism. I saw in Botswana textbooks in biology, where there were species of animals and plants that grow in North America, not Africa. I still remember that outside the ministry of education in Gabarone there were boxes of textbooks given by "bleeding heart liberals" as development aid. They thought these textbooks, produced in Canada, would be useful to children in Botswana. Not to speak of the fact that in Canada they teach in English, instead of in Setsuana, which is the mother tongue of about 60% or 70% of Botswana's population.

Senegal is another interesting country. There were 38 tribal languages, and French was used as the lingua franca. Senegal is interesting for another point as well. It has Gambia as an enclave. Gambia was once taken by the British. Thus English was the language in the school and in the administration. The borders cut across tribes, so they were speaking French here and English there.

Is this a typical situation for the West African coast states?

Oh yes, and there is an unwillingness on the part of the current leaders to admit to this kind of colonialism. Senegal is nothing but a conglomerate of tribes that were conquered by the French. They were not a national entity from the outset.

How would you do international research on the relevance of schooling?

I think the problem of relevancy would have to be looked at from the point of view of the local cultures. There is a very difficult problem here. We are trying to modernize the "underdeveloped" world very rapidly. In this situation, we must remember that, for example, in Scandinavia we did not become so rapidly modernized.

On the other hand, hasn't there developed in these former colonies a distinct upper and middle class eager to attain a liberal European education?

Yes. What you have in these countries is an upper class educated at Harvard, Oxford, or in Paris, which gives them much more in common with the upper class in Europe. The most typical case is India. In contrast, a country that has been able to preserve much of its original culture and identity is Japan.

And the Japanese have at the same time been successful in adapting to the Western model.

In a superficial way — clothing and whatever. In technology they have adapted, even been ahead of the United States. But in terms of the culture in which this is occurring, they have been able to preserve continuity. I thought about a Japanese colleague who took his doctorate in Stockholm in the 1970s. In a way we belonged to the same culture of academics. But when it came to some basic values, we discovered that we were on a different track.

How do you react to the following prediction: During the next, say, 50 years the Asians will take command because of their culture and economic efficiency.

My prediction is that the Asians, whether they are "tigers" or not, will in the first place become economically more successful and therefore more powerful in other respects than the Americans or the Europeans. Whether it will take 50 years or not is another question, but they are coming along very rapidly. In one decade the GNP in Japan more than doubled, which means something like a 6% or 7% increase per year.

Returning to Europe and to national differences, how homogeneous or heterogeneous do you see Europe now?

We were discussing this in the Academia Europea report — to what extent one could think of a kind of unity of European education (Husén, Tuijnanman, and Halls 1992). But with all these languages it is impossible, because each language is part of a culture with several hundred years of tradition. It was quite different in the United States until the turn of this century. Those who were there early had come mainly from Britain, some from Germany; but by and large they were WASPS (White Anglo-Saxon Protestants). Then there was an enormous influx from Eastern and Southern Europe. There were areas full of Italians. Immigrants tend to come in great numbers and settle in certain areas, as did the Scandinavians in the Midwest. But the Americans have been able to establish, particularly through the school system, an American national identity and pride, which is not possible to do in Europe because of the different nationalities and languages. You can see this now in the former Yugoslavia. When they are no longer kept together by a Tito, all kinds of underlying tensions erupt.

A Finnish colleague suggested reintroducing Latin as a medium of instruction in higher education. In principle, I would say, this is not a bad suggestion. I have in my own library textbooks in Latin that were used at the University of Paris in the 17th century. Most of the teaching in the leading universities in Europe at that time was done in Latin.

And today's Latin is English?

Yes, because it is now the first foreign language in eight out of 10 European countries.

Would the French accept a further development of this kind?

They are beginning now to accept it, which they didn't before. They are yielding to necessity.

Higher Education Dilemmas

It is claimed that there has been a change from mass to universal higher education. Could you please elaborate on this and how you see the situation at present?

Let me give you just a little bit of historical background. OECD organized a meeting on higher education in Paris in early 1973, and one of the main speakers there was sociologist Martin Trow from Berkeley. He gave the introductory presentation, which was also the main paper. He introduced a new terminology by talking about elite, mass, and universal higher education. Before this event there was no particular taxonomy in this field. Elite higher education was participation of up to 15%, mass higher education up to 50%, and universal higher education over 50%. And what happened, as you know, was the enormous expansion that took place in some countries, such as Sweden and Norway, already in the 1960s. This wave was connected with economic growth. The other wave came more recently. This has become a problem that needs to be looked into because of the massification of the whole system, in the sense of increased bureaucracy and increased sizes of the institutions, not to mention the problem of quality. When I became professor at Stockholm University 43 years ago there were fewer than 3,000 students; now we have somewhere between 30,000 and 35,000. This means many problems of coordination. Big units in education, be it schools or universities, always present certain problems of administration. And sometimes the bureaucracy grows in an uncontrolled way. At the University of Stockholm when I started, we had a maximum of 10 people as administrative personnel. Now there are close to 1,000 people. But if you multiply by 10 (remembering the increase of students), the number should be 100 administrators. There seems not to be any proportionality between the size of the enrollment and the size of the administration.

These are side effects of massification. The main effect is on quality. In 1969-70, when I was asked by the OECD to be part of the team looking into French higher education and its policy guidelines, I spent some time at the Sorbonne seeing the problems of students not finding places to attend lectures. Then they split the University of Paris into many units: Paris 1, Paris 2, Paris 3, etc. New units were located on the periphery. You will find similar phenomena in many countries.

The Americans coped with the problems in another way. Higher education is more or less a market. There is no federal university. They have a public and private sector in each state of the country. But within the public sector you have differentiation between community colleges, state colleges, and full-size universities. Over the last 20 years it is the two-year community colleges and the four-year colleges that have been growing, though this is not well known. The full-scale universities have not grown much. Their total enrollment in 1996 is about the same as it was in the early 1970s. That was also a period, by the way, when they had to recruit an enormous army of university teachers. Everybody who took a Ph.D. was immediately put to teaching as an assistant professor. This is now a headache, because most of them are going to retire within little more than a decade or so. In many disciplines they are not always sure of finding people who can replace those who retire.

Thinking about the structural pattern of higher education today, do you find similarities all over the world?

What has happened internationally also applies to both Norway and Sweden. A large number of institutions of tertiary education have grown up without being equipped to live up to the research ideals of the Humboldt University. We used to call them subsidiaries (*filialer*) in Sweden. They were under the supervision of the universities. In the 1960s we got subsidiaries in many places, such as Linkøping, Umeå, and Karlstad; and these subsidiaries were for only undergraduates. Another feature of the new institutions was that rather few among the teaching staff had taken doctorates in the disciplines they represented. We got a new kind of university teacher, namely adjuncts, who now dominate

In 1970 Torsten Husén received an honorary doctorate from the University of Rhode Island. University President Frank Newman confers the honor.

As chair of the National Commission of Education of Botswana, Husén presents the commission's report to Botswana's President Sir Serestse Khama (right), while Minister of Education Morake looks on.

*Torsten Husén and his wife Ingrid find themselves in the middle of an
animated discussion with Nobel Prize Laureate Theodore Schultz (left)
of the University of Chicago and U.S. Ambassador to Sweden Kennedy-
Minott (right). The occasion was a reception at the Royal Swedish
Academy of Sciences in connection with the Nobel Prize festivities in
December 1979.*

this institution. They usually have only the basic degrees, a bachelor's or master's. Therefore you cannot expect the teaching in these institutions to be of the same level as in the universities, where you have people teaching who have completed their doctorate or are active in research.

You said earlier that historically you have had teachers with a Ph.D. in the gymnasium. *It seems like a paradox that in tertiary education there are rather few with the highest academic qualification. Do you still have people with Ph.D. degrees in the* gymnasium?

In principle, yes. When I say in principle, I mean according to the regulations there are still positions for those with an advanced degree, licentiate and doctor's degree, at the *gymnasium* in Sweden. But what has happened is, of course, paradoxical, as you pointed out. We are talking sometimes about the "gymnasification" of higher education in Sweden, which is what has taken place. Let me give you the following example. When I came to Lund in 1935 to study history, I went to see the professor. I was 19 then. He gave me a list of books that I was supposed to read on my own. He addressed me as "candidate." At that time this was the title the students had, Mr. Candidate. "Go home, Mr. Candidate, and read these books," he said. I have forgotten how many thousands of pages it was. He continued: "Come back in a year, and we can discuss. In the meantime, you can, of course, attend my seminars. I would appreciate it if you attended them, but it is not compulsory." In practice it was, of course, in spite of what he said. But the emphasis was on independent study. There was a rather high failure rate because many were not able to study on their own. They were used to being spoon-fed. Those who were not used to working independently or who were not intellectually mature enough to work on their own failed. But now we have a system legislated in 1958. By increasing the volume of teaching, the ambition was to improve the situation, and in a way it did. It reduced the dropout rate. But on the other hand, it was, as I put it earlier, a "gymnasification" of the university. The university got many features of a school, which is something quite different from a university. At a genuine university, you study and learn through your own responsibility. In a school, you are taught. That is a big difference.

Does what you are saying imply that Swedish tertiary education has become less elite than it was, that it has become broadened in a way?

The elite is always there, even when there is massification. If by elite you mean, say, the top 5% or 10%, they are still there today; but the intellectual atmosphere is not at the same level of analytical and independent critical study as it was.

The environment at the university has changed. However, I would expect that the elite always find ways to break away from the masses. What sort of "break-away" tendencies do you see in Sweden now?

It is difficult to say. It is now 15 years since I retired, and I haven't been close enough to recent developments. But behind this question about the existence of an elite there is another consideration, namely that the upper secondary school, the *gymnasium*, also has been massified. They used to have more independent studies. You cannot expect the same average IQ level when you have 75% of an age cohort, compared to when you had only 5%. So it is a new situation, which is affected both by the fact that we will soon have almost universal upper secondary education; and we have increased or are in the process of increasing the number who take tertiary education.

What are the new institutions in Sweden, the "subsidiaries," formally called?

They are not called subsidiaries anymore. They are called university colleges. They cooperate with the university. As colleges they are now independent, while before they were under the supervision of one of the universities.

What is the main difference between the university colleges in Sweden and the community colleges in the United States?

In the first place, the community colleges are under the local school board of the community. They cover two, not four, years and they do not grant degrees. The new institutions in Sweden have their own boards. Furthermore, since they are no longer under supervision of the mother university, they can, at least formally, provide the same level of qualifications. On the other hand, one has to notice that they begin to exhibit what the Americans call "academic drift," which means they have started to build up institutions and open up graduate programs. In the beginning they could not award any degrees, now they can. The first step was the basic degree, similar to the bachelor's degree. And then they were able, by permission of the university chancellor, to award master's degrees. They have started to establish university chairs and professorships by getting money from business and industry in their particular field or elsewhere. That is similar to academic drift in American institutions of higher education.

Having these U.S. and Swedish developments in mind, and taking a glance at other parts of the world, do you find many similarities?

Yes, in Australia, though I don't claim to be an expert on Australia. I visited there at the invitation of the ministry of education or department of education in Canberra a few times. In the beginning, Australia's institutions of higher learning were subsidiaries to the British. In order to get both the basic and the advanced degrees, you went to Britain. Then they established their own system and began awarding degrees. In 1971, when I was there for the first time and visited the universities, I think there were a half-dozen. Then they started institutions that the British call polytechnics, and they also had a problem of academic drift. Australia is a parallel, in a way, to France, where they have established two-year studies, particularly in technical fields. This took off strongly in the 1950s and 1960s and was something similar, in terms of the level of quality or competence, to the American community colleges.

In Germany they established what they called *fachhochschulen*, where they had all kinds of vocationally oriented programs already at the tertiary level. Ulrich Teichler, for instance, who is the leading researcher in higher education in Germany, has been working at the *gesamthochschule* in Kassel. In the Soviet Union, the system was different from Central Europe. They had a university system without research, similar to the French. Research in France was conducted in the institutions under the ministry of education. In the Soviet Union it was mainly under the academies. The Soviet Academy had most of the research institutions under its umbrella.

What about Japan?

I'm rather familiar with Japanese higher education. I spent some time in Kyoto back in 1983, going through the entire Japanese education system. The leading Japanese universities were established around the turn of the century. They sent delegations to Europe to pick up the best ideas. So they took the idea of elite institutions from France. The University of Tokyo and the University of Kyoto became the two main so-called imperial universities. The Japanese also looked at ideas about administration and were intrigued by the German model of university administration.

Turning to the future of higher education, or more specifically of the university, what changes do you see or expect?

What we have noticed over the last couple of decades is the enormous increase of enrollment. The institutions have grown explosively. How we are going to cope with this is, in my view, a headache. It depends to some extent on what we feel the main goals of the university should be. Are these institutions mainly there in order to prepare students for certain professional fields, or are they also there to provide general education in a changing society?

So the admission may be changing the function?

In the first place, we have changed the admission system. In Sweden we now have three different criteria for admission. One is having completed secondary education. Then there is admission on the basis of scholastic aptitude tests. And third is admission on the basis of so-called work experience.

In Sweden and Scandinavia, do you foresee any changes in financing universities or in the role of the state in funding the students' fees and so forth?

Given the massification and the fact that most of those who are going to universities cannot be supported by their families, and given the rising costs in various respects, I think that some kind of public scholarships and loans will have to be there. We have a system now, as in Norway, where you can take a loan of a certain sum per year. Part of this is a subsidy, which is dependent on whether you complete the studies or not and the time it takes.

How do you look on the future development of the organization, leadership, and administration of the universities?

In Sweden we got a university frame law in 1975, followed by another law in 1977, which introduced a new system of governance. This system called for representatives of various interest groups on the boards of the universities. Another law came in 1993. The Americans, I think, have found a better model. They have on the university boards people who are recognized as experienced and insightful, and who do not represent any interest groups, at least not formally. We had on our board in Stockholm a representative from LO, another represented the Students' Union, a third represented the Union of the University Teachers, and so on.

There are new tendencies when it comes to governance. For a long time the Rector (the President) was *primus inter pares*, first among equals. He did not have any particular influence, nothing in comparison with the American university president, who is a

116

kind of chief executive officer. Of course, the governance becomes much more difficult in an institution that Clark Kerr has referred to as the "multiversity."

Do you think it is likely that the Scandinavian rector will be transformed into a chief executive officer in the future?

The recent changes that took place in Swedish universities during the time when Per Unckel was minister of education were in the American direction. This led to another composition of the governing boards, and more power was given to the president.

What do you think will happen to the role and status of the professoriate in the future?

There has already been a change. In Scandinavia we had the German model that, in a book that came out in the 1970s, I referred to as "professorial feudalism." Then you had only one professor, the *ordinarius*, in each subject field, and you had the docents, who didn't have tenure. They were appointed for one to three years at a time. In 1960 in Sweden we introduced a new category of teaching staff, the lecturers. In principle, they should have a doctoral degree in the subject they were teaching. At the same time, in our research projects we were using graduate students as teaching assistants for other students. In the United States a professor gives a lecture to an audience of several hundred students. After the lecture, the students are split up in smaller groups, each with its own instructor. Instructor is the word they use. The German model has not survived in the "massified" university.

But I think we have to make clear what we mean by higher education. For instance, the Austrian economist Fritz Machlup, who came to the United States in the early 1930s, asked the question: "Higher education — higher than what?" It is a good question. My ideal university would be one where practically all who are teaching have a doctorate and have demonstrated familiarity with what is said to be the core of academic activities, namely doing analytical, critical work. Furthermore, they also must possess a certain overview of their particular field. What worries me when I look at the situation in Sweden is the "adjuncts" at the new institutions of higher education. They are perhaps one book ahead of those they are teaching. I have suggested recently in the journal of the Swedish University Teacher's Association that everybody who is achieving a Ph.D. of acceptable quality should be offered an assistant professorship in their department or in another university.

Do you think they should have tenure?

No, without tenure. With this opportunity, they should show they are worthy of promotion primarily by their research but also by their teaching. After the three-year period, they are up for review to see if what they have done is regarded as a good contribution to the field. Then they should be given tenure and become associate professors. A certain number of years later, they could be considered for the pool of professorships. This is the American model, which I think has worked very well.

Thinking about the research policies of a university, we have seen different models in the former Soviet Union/Eastern Europe and Western Europe/United States. In the East, universities were primarily education institutions, and research took place in separate academies. In the West, both education and research took place within the university. I wonder if we may expect an Eastern development in the West now — more and more research taking place outside the universities?

What you are referring to here is really what we in Sweden call sector research. This area has been growing recently. Before 1960 there were very few institutions conducting sector research. Especially in certain industries — for example, electronics and pharmaceutics — research is being performed independent of an education program.

118

Do you expect this development to increase?

Yes, but I don't know to what extent. One has the problem of not being in touch with the development of scholarship as in university research. Industry's researchers are more isolated than the university's. Universities have international exchanges and conferences. They also are stimulated by new blood coming in through the graduate students. It is difficult to predict what is going to happen in this area.

There also may be unexpected effects from affirmative action. Under the current mandate the Swedish universities are expected to prefer women for vacant professorships. An interesting thing is, however, that a study has been done on the extent of discrimination against women when filling academic positions, primarily professorships, and it shows that discrimination did not take place to the extent purported.

That was in Sweden?

Yes, the authors were Ulla Riis and Leif Lindberg. They did an empirical study on how professorships were granted (1996). I also looked into one aspect of this field and found no discrimination: It was about the number of women in science. In a memorandum I wrote for the U.S. National Academy of Sciences in 1993, I found that the number of female Ph.D.'s varied enormously in the different natural sciences. In physics it was about 10%; in chemistry it was higher, some 20%; and in biology it was 40%. This corresponds very much to the findings of the IEA studies of girls taking science at the upper secondary level.

Why are there so few women in science?

In the 1970s I had a doctoral student, Allison Kelly, a sociologist from Britain who took her doctoral degree with a thesis on "Girls and Science." Her original theory was that sex differences in science test scores were due to sociocultural factors. The problem was that in practically all countries there was a similar pattern. The sex differences in performance increased from age 10 to age 18. This also applied to social classes within different countries. There was a big sex difference in Japan and Chile, as in Sweden, England, and the United States. I don't maintain that the explanation is genetic, but there may be something connected to heredity. The fact is, Kelly was not able to show that strong sociocultural determinants fully explain sex differences in science performance.

Thinking about the research done by women at the universities, is it fair to say that the more notable research by women has been in the social sciences? Has this something to do with feminist interests?

I'm not quite sure that they have been most successful in the social sciences. My impression is that they have been most successful in the humanities. There they have a higher percentage on the faculty. We now have quite a few female professors in Stockholm, for example, in philology — in the philology of foreign languages — or in literature. There are not so many in the social sciences.

What do you think about feminist claims of having brought up a new paradigm in the Kuhnian sense of scientific research?

I can express this very briefly. I'm strongly skeptical because this represents a kind of epistemological relativism that I think is dangerous. I'm skeptical about the notion of a research approach by nature because gender is something by nature. I have met these claims in connection with the preparation of the *International Encyclopedia of Education*, where I was the co-editor-in-chief, and where we now have a section on gender.

To what degree do you see a delicate grey zone between feminist research and social policy struggles of equity and justice between the genders?

If I look back on research from the mid 1940s up to now that has to do with equality of opportunity in education, I cannot find that men have played any more prominent role than women. There are major contributions by both sexes. Maybe women are closer to what is referred to as "bleeding heart liberals" than men are? Recently on Swedish television, the national chairperson of the Social Democratic Women's Association suggested that all top positions in the public sector in Sweden, up to 2,000, should be filled with women because women were more reliable in the sense of not being so "scandalous," as you know some of the top males have been.

What is your comment on some female social scientists' claim that women more than men are dominated by a caring rationality, while men are dominated by an instrumental rationality?

Well, it is a fact that women are more caring than men, that is obvious. But when it is about caring rationality, this is another matter and depends on how you define rationality. I'm skeptical on that point, as well.

It seems as though the traditional Humboldt-inspired university is changing in the direction of what some people are calling service universities, meaning that the university has to act more like a company in a market, having to sell research or knowledge-based services to generate sufficient revenues for its needs. What do you think about this development?

Traditionally the university trained professionals, most of them for public service as priests, doctors, lawyers, and teachers. These are the main categories.

I still remember the first conference we had in Aspen, Colorado, back in the early 1970s, where we were discussing the role of the university. We talked about teaching, research, and service to society. Americans have a special tradition in the 1862 Land Grant Colleges Act (the Morrill Act). Universities were given land for providing teaching, and partly research, that would improve agriculture and industry in the United States. What has happened recently in Europe, not least in Scandinavia, is that the universities, particularly the new ones, are supposed to be a kind of service to the business and industry in a particular region. One has questioned their usefulness. But in periods when securing necessary funds is difficult, they are beginning to obtain money from the surrounding society. Therefore they get involved in paid services. As I mentioned earlier, strong efforts are being made to obtain grants establishing new professorships, particularly professorships that are service-oriented.

In principle, all this was dealt with in the early 1960s by Clark Kerr, when he gave his famous series of lectures at Harvard University, published in his book, *The Uses of the University* (1963). The whole idea of the service university has been much more in the forefront in the United States than in Europe. I still remember when I was a graduate student at the university, service was considered degrading, a kind of treason against academic values by its concentration on the "useful." You were a professor in the university in order to search for truth, and it was considered corrupting to have a contract with a company or sometimes even a governmental agency. Over the years I often have been in the situation of doing research paid by a grant from the school board of Stockholm, the National Board of Education, or from a governmental commission. In this situation, it is self-evident that you are asked to do certain things and investigate particular problems. But it is up to you the way you pose problems, collect information, analyze data, and report findings. It is then up to them to interpret what they want to interpret. I do not think such services corrupt the idea of the university.

Speaking of the development of the service university in the United States, do you see major differences between American public and private universities? Is their market situation different?

Public universities in the United States are not dependent on the market to the same extent as private ones, even though both private and public institutions get money through fundraising drives and contributions from private persons and companies. A famous example is Stanford University. There were once two students at

Stanford who had ideas. One was Hewlett; the other was Packard. They started their business in the garage just outside Stanford campus somewhere back in the 1930s. As you know, Hewlett-Packard has become a world leader in certain electronic products. They later gave enormous sums of money to Stanford. But I think the Stanford University leadership was careful in selecting the sort of donations they would accept. Stanford was offered an enormous amount of money to establish a Reagan Library. For some reason the faculty was not very enthusiastic about Reagan, so Stanford didn't accept the grant. This example illustrates how a market-based private university refused a particular offer for reasons of independence. The point I am driving at here is that it is important to protect academic autonomy. Nobody should be able to influence the researcher in terms of methods or use of data, just to please the one who gave you the grant.

Given that we cannot avoid a service university development in Scandinavia, how will institutional autonomy be preserved?

As I said before, when you begin a study you should be free to frame the problems, select and process the data, and report it in your own way. I have seen this in connection with UNESCO and the International Institute of Educational Planning (IIEP) when a study in some African countries was conducted during the first years of its existence. The study turned out to be very embarrassing for the ministry of education in one African country, and the IIEP administration was contacted by Maheu, who wanted to repress the report. He was then the director general of UNESCO. There was a fight about this, which was won by IIEP in the UNESCO General Conference in 1968.

How would you argue for a strong economic foundation for the research university?

In the first place this is important for quality, and secondly for independence and autonomy. It is important that there are basic resources for the university. The private American universities, such as Stanford and Harvard, have endowments; and the interests from the endowments keep them running up to a certain level, but usually they need extra.

From Adult Education to Lifelong Learning

What's the situation of adult education in terms of quality?

My first contact with adult education in Sweden was with the extension activities, in terms of lectures given outside the University of Lund. There were so-called local lecture associations, which were associated with the popular movements, such as temperance. I gave lectures about war propaganda from 1941 through 1944. At the same time students at the University of Lund were hired to lead study circles. Such activities had started seven to eight years earlier in Stockholm around 1933. This may be a typical Swedish activity, I am not quite sure. In the early part of the 20th century the first study circles were established and called "Group of Companions Getting Together." Nobody was in the authoritarian position of deciding what should be taught and how. One of the participants was elected to lead the circle. And so university students got involved. This meant in 1947 that a national association was formed, called *Folkuniversitetet*, which had extramural departments in Stockholm, Gothenburg, Lund, and Uppsala.

In 1952 I became a board member of the department of the "folk university" in Stockholm. I had some experience from Lund, having conducted study circles there at the workers' movement. Later, after I was appointed to the professorship in education at Stockholm University, they thought, who could be more knowledgeable than the new professor of education; and so I was appointed chairman of the governing board, and elected "inspector" as well. It was a kind of dual role. Since the folk university was connected to the university, the university needed somebody who would ensure they were following the rules. This was in 1953, and I couldn't foresee then that I would have this appointment until 1973. I resigned when I went for a sabbatical year to

Stanford. In the meantime I had been elected chairman of the board of the entire folk university of Sweden. I succeeded Torgny Segerstedt, who was the first chairman and who resigned because he had been elected rector to the University of Uppsala.

There was another contact of a more professional character that I had with adult education in Sweden, namely through the adult education seminar. There were some people in the study associations of the workers' movement, templar movement, free church movement, and so on, who wanted to encourage the pedagogical aspect and even the research aspect of adult education. So they took the initiative to establish an adult education seminar at Stockholm University. From 1953 on we had regular seminar sessions on adult education. You can find in the Bibliography that I wrote about it in the journal of the folk university at its 10-year anniversary (1963). The participants in the seminar were the top people within the various study associations, those who (using a bad translation into English) would be called "study rector" and "study secretary," respectively. We had a set topic for each seminar; it could be a topic related to didactic problems. One topic over the series of seminar sessions was how adults learn. From these experiences came a book called *Adult Learning* (*Vuxna Lär*), which came out in 1958 and was later reissued in many editions. The seminar played an important role in connecting this activity, which was heavily subsidized by tax money, to the academic sphere. Many of the people in the study association had to move upward, so to speak, both socially and in other respects. They had a kind of inherited skepticism of the academic world.

There were two things we did in the seminar. We prepared this book that came out, and we dealt with problems central to adult education in Sweden. The interesting thing is that in Sweden at that time adult education was a means of recruiting spokesmen for the popular movements or associations. It was, in principle, not for the individual to make a career. It was even regarded as inappropriate to take courses that promoted your own career and made you earn more money. That would have been seen as a kind of treason against your own class, particularly in the workers'

125

movement. I'll give you an example. Olof Palme chaired a government committee on student aid. He came up with the idea that those who did not have the opportunity to get advanced formal education ought to be given one. His committee proposed setting up a system whereby those adults who by the age of 20 would like additional formal (secondary) education could have a chance for further individual development. Because of this initiative, something called Municipal Adult Education (KOMVUX, the Swedish acronym) was created. The interesting thing is that there were quite a few people in the workers' movement who opposed the idea, saying, "This is nothing for us." There was one particular man, a leader in the workers' movement, who called the lack of formal schooling a "lucky injustice." The lucky injustice was that, since his people did not have the opportunity to move up the ladder of formal education, they could use their ability and competence to promote the workers' movement. At that time there was a governmental commission that in 1961 submitted a report suggesting even more support and extended activities in adult education, supported by the state or by the municipalities. The municipalities supported formal education, but they didn't support study circle activities. The big item in the state education budget was the study circle. There were some rules in order to get public financial support. For instance, there had to be at least five people in the circle.

At that time there also was an interest in adult education from the point of view of a changing society. In 1961 I published a book called *The School in a Changing Society*, which was attacked by the conservatives. In the first place they denied that society was changing, and second, they disliked my conclusion that the school had to concentrate on basic skills, particularly how to learn, which was at the center of what the school should do. This was the kind of philosophy I tried to inject into the 1957 committee that worked on the preparation of the comprehensive nine-year school, and then later on the *gymnasium* committee in 1960. Palme, by the way, was one of the members of that committee. So some of us began to think in terms of what was referred to as continuing education. I had learned about it in the United States when I visited the centers for continuing education at several universities. In Europe one began in the 1960s to talk about continuing education, which later changed to lifelong education.

Was the term recurrent education *also used?*

Yes, in the late 1960s we began in Scandinavia to talk about recurrent education (*återkommande utbilding*). I remember Palme once asked me what the appropriate term could be, and I suggested recurrent education. Some time later, in 1969, he gave a keynote speech in a meeting outside Paris and used that term. So in OECD at the end of 1960s, recurrent education was the buzzword of the day. And I remember that in 1969 OECD established their so-called strategy group, of which I became a member. Another member was, by the way, an unknown person from Britain, Margaret Thatcher. The group was expected to suggest OECD guidelines for education policy. In 1973 OECD appointed a task force, chaired by Clark Kerr. One member was Jacques Delors. I was asked to join. We dealt with the problem of transition from school to work, but we could not avoid dealing with this problem of "continuing" or "permanent" education as well. *Permanent education* was yet another term. What you find now when you look at the OECD documents or at the recent Delors Report is that they speak very eloquently about *lifelong education* (1996). But this has already been discussed for a long time, perhaps in a more confused intellectual atmosphere than the present one. Now we are used to a society that is in rapid change, where the economy goes up and down. It is not going up all the time as it did in the 1960s. It was impossible to predict what would come, but in the late 1960s we were trying to figure out how education would look by the year 2000. We based our assumptions on the socioeconomic idea that there would be continuous increase.

Thinking about a phrase you used a little while ago, "lucky injustice," could one say that the success of the Swedish school reform also had a dysfunctional effect on the working class' opportunity to produce their own leaders? In other words, has the end of "lucky injustice" meant "brain drain" and reduced power for the working class as such?

What has happened is that social mobility has been promoted by these various education reforms. The lucky injustice was that you were locked into your own class. I noticed as late as 1954 in Stockholm, when you still could move from grade 4 in the primary school to grade 1 of the secondary academic track, to what the British would call the "grammar school," that those with working-class background in Stockholm did not really take advantage of the opportunity. The schools were the same distance from their homes. There were no fees. Those with a working-class background who had high grades and were qualified to get into the grammar schools in many cases simply did not enter. They didn't take advantage because such an education did not "belong" culturally to their class. In some instances those from working-class background who chose to take the opportunity of continuing in an academic track were seen as traitors to their own class. The genetic background may have played a role here. Relatively, it seems to cause more and more importance, the more equal conditions there are in the society where one grows up. So the more effective the system is in giving an opportunity to those who have the ability to take advantage of it, the more brain drain there is "down there."

How do you think this development may influence the solidarity culture of our societies?

Michael Young once wrote a book about the rise of meritocracy. We spent quite a lot of time together in the United States back in 1978 on behalf of OECD looking at the education of the disadvantaged. He tried to describe the consequences of a selection system, which he thought created a meritocratic society.

Michael Young's work became a cult book of that time. Do you know anything about his background, professional training, and experience?

He had taken his doctorate in sociology. I forget whether it was in Oxford or Cambridge. He came up by getting a stipend that enabled him to continue academic schooling. For some time he was the research director for the British Labour Party. I was introduced to him by Anthony Crosland, then British minister of education. Anthony Crosland's father was a top civil servant in the War Office during World War II. He went to a private, independent school. Crosland and Young met, I would guess in Oxford, because Anthony Crosland was teaching economics there. Michael Young wrote his book on meritocracy at the Center for Advanced Studies at Stanford University back in the late 1950s.

He became quite famous because of the book.

Yes. It was translated into Swedish. It was called *Inteligensen som Överklass*, literally *Intelligence as Upper Class*, in a way a better title for its content. He coined the word *meritocracy*. It is a very good term.

Did he have other important contributions?

No and yes. This is the book that became famous. He wrote a few other studies, but I must confess that I do not recall the later works by him. But he played an important role in this debate.

Margaret Thatcher and Decentralization

Earlier you mentioned your encounter with Margaret Thatcher. Both as British minister of education and as prime minister in the United Kingdom, she was much concerned about the education policies of her country. "Educational Thatcherism" is sometimes used. How do you assess her education policy?

As far I can remember now, she attended only one of the meetings of the so-called strategy group in Paris. And then she faded away. Apparently she didn't think of our work as something particularly important.

Was she minister of education then?

When we met she had just succeeded Anthony Crosland from Labour. I knew Crosland from several visits during the latter part of the 1960s. I met Margaret Thatcher again after many years in March 1993. Typically, Margaret Thatcher was an honorary fellow of the Hoover Institution at Stanford. It was established as a kind of conservative think tank, which was, of course, a problem because most of the other people in the academic community at Stanford, particularly the social scientists, were more liberal — or more radical, whatever you would like to call it. Anyway, she was there. So we had a breakfast meeting with some 75 to 100 people. Margaret Thatcher was telling us what was right and what was wrong. She was like a school mistress or a school principal, and very sharp. The interesting thing was that most of the changes toward comprehensive education in Britain took place during her time as minister of education. Very little happened during that Labour government.

She wanted to centralize the British education system. The school system was by tradition extremely decentralized, and the 150 or so local education authorities (LEAs) had the power. The minister of education and his (or her) staff had very little to say except for the influence that was exerted by the inspectors. They were called Her Majesty's Inspectors. But the real power was with the local education authorities. Thatcher wanted to give schools the possibility to opt out of the local education authorities.

Centralization has occurred in terms of preparing curriculum and having national assessments. British teachers reacted strongly against the reforms. Paradoxically, Thatcher's reforms made it possible for the central agency, in this case the ministry, to exert influence. If it was in charge of the national assessment and also in charge of drawing up the general framework for the curriculum, it exerted considerable power. Previously there were just some curriculum guidelines, a framework. On one hand there was centralization, on the other decentralization in certain aspects, at least in terms of governance. That is to say, there is centralization in terms of content, what the goals are and what should be taught, and decentralization in terms of how it should be done.

Margaret Thatcher also wanted to give the parents more power because school bureaucracy, particularly in the local education authorities, had taken more and more control.

There were a lot of complaints from the teacher trade unions about Thatcher's centralization policies. But if you compare the level of centralization in England and Sweden, wouldn't Sweden still be more centralized than England?

Yes. You have to consider how one is defining centralization or decentralization. In England, the spread in pupil achievements between schools in terms of average level is about three times as large as in Norway or Sweden. The United States also has a large spread, but there one has much more ethnic diversity.

How do you explain this difference between the United Kingdom and the Scandinavian countries?

When I'm talking about the spread now, I'm talking about the IEA studies conducted in the 1960s and 1970s, before any Thatcherism had made its appearance. The spread, I would guess, has been reduced by the new reforms in the United Kingdom, which in a way is good because you find a higher percentage of the total school population in Britain performing very badly compared to many other European countries.

There has been both in England and in Scandinavia a general wave of decentralization during recent years. Why do we have this change in attitude, and what is the level of decentralization really carried out?

I think it has to do with the growth of school bureaucracies. I used to refer to the number of pages of regulations that have been issued by the central government. How many pages of regulations were there in 1995 as compared, say, to 1895 or 1905 or 1925? It has been growing all the time. In order to see to it that these regulations are followed, you need people. At the same time, there has been an enormous increase of other nonteaching staff, not only those who are in the ministries or other agencies, but those who are performing special tasks, such as psychologists, social workers, and nurses. When I was growing up, there were 3,000 municipalities in Sweden. In my municipality there were about 2,000 to 3,000 people and four schools. At best the schools had one head teacher. The rest of the staff were teachers, and they had no other function. The teachers were teaching also at the upper levels. Now Sweden has less than 300 municipalities. In each of these we have all kinds of people doing all kinds of things. Before 1950 Sweden had one central bureaucracy in Stockholm, with several hundred people in charge of planning and revising the curriculum and inspecting. There were also regional inspectors, a system that was introduced in Sweden in each of the 24 counties more than 100 years ago. I can remember from my own school time only once, or maybe twice, that an inspector turned up.

So, if you ask me, the urge for decentralization has to do with the fact that there is more competence at the local level than in the past. The people who know how to do things and who have professional competence were previously concentrated in the capital of the country. On the other hand, there is an interest in centralizing — centralizing in the meaning of stating the goals and the framework for the curricula. In most countries nowadays, curricula are prepared in the ministry of education, and sometimes even passed in the parliament, and then issued as prescriptions by the government. So the need for decentralization also has to do with the growth of the system as such.

There have been debates on whether a real transfer of power from the center to the local level has occurred. What do you think?

It is a good question. As I said, I used to point to the number of pages of regulations, and I do not know how thick the volume of regulations is now. You have the school law, and then you have certain regulations based on the school law, issued by either the government or the national board of education. So, in certain respects, I think there is less marginal freedom at the local level than before.

Why?

Because in order to get money from the government, you have to fulfill certain obligations and live up to certain rules. So the government is very powerful. But there is more freedom left now, at least formally, to the local schools. I have noticed that the schools in Sweden have much more local freedom in how to organize teaching activities than before.

Do they use the opportunity of selecting their own content?

Yes, but they are very hesitant because for centuries they have been used to following central directives. I still remember when, I forget in what context, it was left to the schools to do certain things. The schools began to call the Stockholm national board of education to ask if they were allowed to do this and that. They were actually asking for directives.

In terms of school leadership, have you noticed particular changes?

My observation is that while previously principals were pedagogical leaders, nowadays they are a kind of manager. When I was in the upper secondary school, we were 500 students. The principal in that school had 10 periods per week of teaching. He had some assistance by one of the teachers in conducting office duties, but he did not even have a regular secretary. That was all. If you go to a school in Sweden now with 500 students, you probably find a group of three to five administrative staff, including a full-time secretary to the principal. You will find a study director under the principal, and even one or two others who are in charge of certain personnel matters. There are more regulations and more formalities that have to be attended to. You have the problem of bureaucratization of the entire system, which makes the principal a manager. My granddaughter tells me that she has not even seen the principal at her school. He is apparently sitting in his office all the time. So my overall impression is that there is an exodus from pedagogy to management.

The War of the Professions and the Status of Schools

Do you think that the army of specialists from the different professions who now help the teachers have actually proved dysfunctional for the school?

In a way, all kinds of professional aspects of pedagogical leadership have been taken over by specialists. Nowadays no one takes care of the "whole" pupil. Since there are all kinds of specialists, the individual pupil is divided into sections, one for teaching; one for the physical well-being, taken care of by the nurse and the doctor; and one for the psychological well-being, of which the school psychologists or social workers are in charge.

Is this development a worldwide trend, or is it a Scandinavian welfare state problem?

All advanced countries nowadays are more or less welfare states. I have noticed the same trend in the United States. I have visited many schools there, and I noticed how big they are, particularly at the secondary level. I think size is a main part of the problem. I mean, by and large, the development is the same all over the world. We in Scandinavia may have become Americanized earlier than our counterparts in the rest of Europe.

The principal is, of course, a key factor in any school. From your research and experiences, do you see any distinct differences in the function, status, and authority of the principal around the world? In particular, what about Japan?

My impressions are rather superficial. In terms of Japan, and this applies to many sectors of the Japanese society, the person formally in charge is in charge. One also has to note that becoming a principal is less prestigious now than it was before. The teaching profession also is less prestigious. But I cannot pass any judgment about what happened in various parts of the world.

You mentioned lower prestige for the teaching profession. Does that also imply less interest in and prestige for schooling in general?

No, because in modern society the more schooling you have, the greater your chance of upward social mobility or of increasing your income. In 1970 I made an interesting observation. Ingvard Carlsson, then minister of education in Sweden, was the keynote speaker at an OECD policy conference. One of his main points was that now that young people had gotten their fair share of education as a common good, it was time for the adults. In the early 1980s there was another meeting. Irrespective of whether they served socialist or conservative governments, they said: "Now we have to begin to save because things are becoming so expensive." The cost per student per year had grown by 200% to 300% in many countries, including our own.

Have you made any comparison of budgets in terms of changes in relative portions for different sectors, education compared, for example, to health and other areas?

OECD has published statistics about this. The general trend has been that schooling has been increasing its share of the GNP. I am talking about formal schooling now. The increase for age 18 or 19 has stopped, whereas for higher education and research the increase goes on. Another point I mentioned in a paper written a few years ago is how many of those who vote in general elections have children of school age. I found that in Germany, at a given point, 40% of the voters had either their own children or closely related children in school. That was cut in half when the birth rate went down, from 40% to a little bit more than 20% of the voters. This affected the public's priorities in relation to schooling compared with other areas of public expenditure.

135

The prestige of the teaching profession is decreasing, but the status of schooling is generally high or increasing. Has this seeming contradiction any connections to the status of private schooling?

In some countries, such as Sweden, it was considered something like swearing in church to speak about privatizing education. I felt this to be very dogmatic, though I have never had a particular love for private education, particularly because most Swedes would not be able to pay for it. It would be only for the very rich. But recently, there has been new legislation on the so-called free schools. It allows independent or private schools that follow the public school curriculum and timetable, and the goals that set the framework, to have most of their expenses covered by the state.

Are you talking about the school voucher system?

Yes. It was very difficult to have this system introduced in America because public education was regarded as the backbone of American democracy. Schools were established in the United States, as pointed out earlier, by local initiative, not by legislation. They were above all not legislated by the federal government. So, it was a very tough issue until they began to find deficits in the efficiency of the public sector. In Minnesota, for instance, they recently began an experiment with vouchers. As long as they can show that privatization can enhance efficiency by using money better and satisfying the parents and students, then it works. I can give you one example. When Coleman published his study on public and private schools in the early 1980s, he became the target of an enormous amount of criticism from those who did not want to accept the facts. At that time 8% to 9% of the students in the United States went to private schools, most of them parochial schools run by the Catholic community. Coleman showed, keeping background in terms of economic conditions under control, that they performed better and were cheaper than public schools. Why? Because the teachers in these schools were satisfied with a lower salary than what is recommended by the American Federation of Teachers, to which many public school teachers belong. This kind of experience favored the voucher system.

The Curriculum and School Excellence

Have you noticed major tendencies in the ways recent curricula are developed?

In the first place, ambitions have been raised, resulting in attempts to cover more subject fields. More and more different content is taught. I'll give you an example. In 1956 I started a big project on curriculum content, *syllabus* as they call it in English. The subject areas were reading, writing, and mathematics. The first thing that we tried to do was to map out how much emphasis was given to each element in the syllabus. We cooperated with a rather big and representative group of teachers in Sweden. They had to keep a kind of diary on how much time they spent on a given element in Swedish or on algebra. When we looked at the outcomes of this exercise, I said to somebody, "I notice now that the 1919 curriculum has finally entered the classrooms." This syllabus was a very progressive one for its time because it was an outline of a rather progressive curriculum movement. As you can see, change is very slow. What has happened in Sweden in recent years is that they have had one curriculum committee after the other, each assuming that the new curriculum issued could be introduced in the respective schools by the first of July the next year.

What is quality in education?

It is important to operationalize what is meant by quality in education. I recently wrote a memorandum on this for SACO, the Federation of Swedish Academics. They wanted me to spell out what I meant by quality in higher education, but it is the same at any level. I wrote a two-part memorandum, the first on the general principles of assessing quality, the second on operationalizing the criteria to be used. This is the important thing, of course. You also have to assess quality from the point of view of how competence is created. I mean, you can have a very bad intake, say to the course or to the stage in the school system, but you may be able to lift the students to a higher level. This is an indication of good quality of teaching. There are all kinds of operational criteria, for example, the dropout rate, grade-repeating rate, and the factual knowledge that you can test at the end, which in some instances is an important thing.

The attainment of factual knowledge then is the most important indicator of quality education?

Yes, the most important indicator, and perhaps the most objective one.

How did the label "schools of excellence" come up?

The term began to be used in the United States during the first part of the Reagan Administration, in 1981, I think. They appointed the National Commission of Excellence, some 20 people. I met with them in Washington, D.C., a year later. I also met them when they were talking about the necessity of teaching good science at Stanford. I found the general talk about excellence to be quite a lot of rhetoric, as I also found President Bush's getting together all the governors in Capitol Hill in 1989, when they tried to set goals for American school education by the year 2000. I commented on it by writing a critical article for *The European*, called "Making School Reforms by Slogan."

Immigrants and the Nordic Identity

I would like to have your comments on education and the immigration issue, taking Sweden as a starting point. Has recent immigration influenced Swedish education significantly?

Yes, it has. Before 1960, this was not an issue. But in the early 1960s workers immigrated from Southern Europe to Sweden because of the lack of workers in Swedish industry. About half of these first immigrants came mainly from Italy, Yugoslavia, Greece, and Turkey. Half came from Finland. This then raised the issue of the language of instruction. I remember it from the first IEA studies, where we did surveys in mathematics and science, both in the 1960s and around 1970. We found at the later occasion that some 8% to 10% of the children came from homes where Swedish was not the mother tongue. This, as you certainly know, led to legislation about the right of immigrant children to have a certain number of class hours per week in their mother tongue. It also had consequences for the adults. They could attend courses in Swedish on paid working time. In a narrow sense it was a language issue, but in the wider sense the teaching was concerned with cultural issues. Multiculturalism as an issue in Sweden came to the forefront in the 1970s, and the proportion of immigrant children in schools has increased since then. There has been another wave recently in connection with the upheaval in the Balkan countries.

Immigration to Sweden has not been without controversy. Some parents of immigrant children, particularly those who hope to settle down for good in Sweden, think that the extra hours of teaching in their mother tongue can handicap the children in other subjects. They have to leave the regular class in order to have a lesson in their mother tongue.

Employment is highly correlated with the amount of formal education. Lower formal education and unemployment is more frequent among immigrants than among settled Swedish citizens.

How could immigrants be encouraged to take more advantage of the education system to consolidate their positions as new citizens in such countries as Norway and Sweden?

They are encouraged to take what is offered in education. As I said, there was legislation that, on paid working time, you could attend courses in Swedish. But you have the kind of difficulty you find everywhere in the world. Immigrants may face serious integration problems even though they are not discriminated against. They are not readily accepted in the same way that the regular people of a country are. Only now do we have the first one or two members in parliament who come from countries other than Sweden. You find the same problem, for instance, in California. Those at the lowest level in the social system are Mexicans and Hispanics and blacks from the South, who, when agricultural change took place in the South, migrated to industrial areas in the West or East. They became a kind of a new underclass in the new settlement area.

What connection do you see between immigration to Scandinavia and the recent surfacing of neo-Nazism?

In times when job security is reduced, fascist reactions occur. You must remember that the big wave of Nazism in the early 1930s came in the wake of mass unemployment. Everywhere in Europe, both manual workers and the lower middle class were in a very insecure situation. When there is insecurity about employment or "daily bread," there often is the tendency to find scapegoats, whether they be Jews, immigrants, or whatever. This has been studied by the Frankfurter sociologists Horkheimer and Adorno, who published a book on the authoritarian personality (1950). It is a psychological analysis of this phenomenon, how susceptible to Nazism in general and racism in particular, people are. I remember from my youth in the 1930s how negative the Swedes were against immigrants from the Continent.

Before World War II?

Yes. Those who came in then were Germans, and most were Jews. There were also some who came from the political sphere. I still remember the debate about accepting a certain number of German Jewish medical doctors, even in the Students Association, both in Lund and Uppsala. They voted for or against accepting immigrants. Roughly half of them were against, the other half for.

So these attitudes can be interpreted as resistance against foreigners. Racism then is not something new in Scandinavia; perhaps it was just slowing down in the 1950s and 1960s.

Oh, yes, that was a period of full employment. The welfare society was built up. But during periods of insecurity this phenomenon of racism pops up. Also, single individuals with particular personality traits feel attracted to what I would call not so much racism as scapegoatism.

Do you find it fair to talk about a particular Nordic or Scandinavian ethnocentrism?

I think a certain amount of ethnocentrism applies to all nationalities, and I do not think there is a particularly stronger ethnocentrism in our region than in others. We have had a favorable situation of being ethnically rather pure nations. In the schools in Sweden in the 1950s, I think about 1% of the students came from homes where Swedish was not the mother tongue. Now it is about 10% to 12%. If you are ethnically pure, then you feel secure in your environment and have no need to defend or be aggressive to anybody outside.

Do you find it meaningful to talk about a particular Nordic identity?

I talked about that often during the 1950s and 1960s when I was a member of an expert group on education experimentation and research under the Nordic Cultural Commission. During that period a lot of issues were resolved, for example, the abolishing of passports between the Nordic countries. Moving from one Nordic country to another automatically gave you the same rights as citizens in that particular country. The issue of having a common Nordic labor market also was explored. Thus there were many reasons why there was a particularly strong feeling of common identity in the Nordic countries.

I was involved in trying to make the university curricula more compatible. We were not very successful, because universities are difficult to change. However, there was an exchange of experiences in school curricula and attempts at making a common Nordic model of curricula. Also, there were attempts to correct

Spain's King Juan Carlos greets Torsten Husén in 1980. Husén had been involved in a review of higher education in Spain.

A smiling Husén is surrounded by school children on a visit to a Stockholm primary school in 1981.

prejudices and stereotypes in the textbooks. When I was in primary school, I read about all the wars we fought, one after the other from the 1520s, against the bad Danes. We talked about "Christian the Tyrant," who in Denmark was referred to as "Christian the Good" (as Norwegian King he was Christian II, the last defender of the Catholic Church in Norway). There were similar attempts by the Council of Europe to get rid of such prejudices throughout Europe, at least for those who are member states. All the steps taken by the Nordic Cultural Commission contributed to reinforce a Nordic identity.

Several foreigners find the Scandinavian countries more democratic than other countries. What is your opinion?

If we exclude the period 1940 to 1945, we have been in the fortunate situation to live in peaceful separation from the rest of Europe. The establishment of democratic institutions and the maturation of these institutions has not been disturbed by the radical changes that have taken place in many other countries on the Continent.

Do you see historical roots that explain or justify statements about more participation in democratic processes here in Scandinavia?

I think there are. In the first place, things have developed in an orderly fashion. Furthermore, in Scandinavia we have had legislation that made municipalities self-governed. This implied a real decentralization of power. I do not know whether there was similar legislation in Norway in the 19th century. Another important factor is the folk high schools, which spread from Denmark into Norway and Sweden. Many of those who were involved in the municipality councils and became leaders had attended folk high school. We also had other popular movements: the workers' movement, the anti-drinking movement, and there was a free church movement as well. Then, of course, the trade union movement played a central role in the political development in Scandinavia. All these popular movements, often with their own education establishments, constituted the substructure of democracy in our region.

To what degree do you think it is fair to claim that we have passed the peak of participatory democracy and are now going in the other direction toward more stratified and more elitist structures?

It depends how you define democracy. Democracy has a participatory aspect that by definition is very important. For example, you have to cast your vote in general elections. What I see as a problem in Sweden is the reform that brought the number of municipalities down from 3,000 to less than 300. This meant that even at the local level there are certain barriers between citizens and those who sit more or less full time in the decisionmaking bodies. This made democratic processes more complicated. Another aspect that has come into the picture is that we have a meritocratic society, which means that the more competent you are in terms of formal education and in other respects, the better off you are in life. You get higher income, you have more options and more influence. This is what I referred to earlier as a kind of paradox in our democracy. Democratizing education, making it available to all citizens, also seems to create a more meritocratic nation.

Globalization and the United Nations

Globalization *is another buzzword today. In what ways do you see education as having become more international or globalized?*

There are certain, quite obvious globalizing features affecting education today. People travel more, workers migrate more. Student exchange between countries has increased perhaps tenfold over the last decades. The media convey pictures of how things are in other countries. All this opens up the horizon to other parts of the world; and this has, of course, repercussions on education.

I don't know whether you are familiar with John Meyer and his group at Stanford. They are studying the globalization that goes on in education, a kind of *rapprochement* between the various national and regional systems. This is a group I worked with in 1984, when I was visiting professor at Stanford. They were working on the theory that there are links between the education systems of the world. The world is becoming more and more alike in terms of education structure, curriculum, and so on. In a recent seminar I dealt with the fact that we are exporting the Western model of schooling to the rest of the world. There is no doubt that globalization and internationalization of the education system is going on at a rapid speed. In some countries it is even stated as a national goal of education, to make the students more aware of international problems. This has, as you know, been one of the overriding goals of UNESCO — to use education to promote peace and understanding. That was the aim of the first representatives of UNESCO in the late 1940s.

Do you see any problems following from the globalization process of education?

Of course. We dealt with this when we talked about immigration. One feels that the traditions "back home" are threatened, so to speak, by influences from abroad, to the extent that even our own identity is threatened. This is in the report on education for the 21st century, the report that UNESCO commissioned Jacques Delors and his group to submit (1996). Parts of the report deal with both globalization and internationalization of education. They call it international cooperation on education in the "global village."

I see a paradox here. On the one hand, you want people to learn more about other parts of the world to understand each other better and to promote peace. On the other hand, globalization, which has its starting point in the Western cultural model, collides with and overrides local traditions and ways of socializing, especially in the developing countries. So to me, the paradox is this: If I am in charge of the education policies of a developing country, how can I make my people competitive and at the same time grounded in the local culture and local ways of learning? To me this is a dilemma without solution. What do you think?

The model that the United States and other countries who are aiding in education are promoting is coming into conflict with the model that is closely related to the local culture. But I don't see this as an insoluble controversy. In order to be competitive, you have to acquire competencies of a more specific character. However, you also have to get a background in general education. While you are opening up your horizon to all kinds of knowledge, which to a certain extent is common for the whole world, you can also include the history of your own country and culture. It is a problem, but the very fact of acknowledging it as such makes it perhaps more accessible to solutions.

After World War II many people had high expectations of UNESCO. Looking at the organization in retrospect and from your particular knowledge of it, how do you assess its history and its role and significance today?

I am not quite sure that I know enough about what is going on in the secretariat in Paris nowadays. You know, my insight derives mainly from the International Institute for Educational Planning (IIEP) and the Education Department, with which I have had close relationships from the early 1950s.

UNESCO has been promoting science and culture in general. I am hesitant to come up with any particular assessments. I can only make some statements about my impressions related to education. There is no doubt about UNESCO's important achievements. I am judging from the general conferences I have attended, and I think that what UNESCO has been doing in education and planning has been very highly appreciated. They have trained planners from all the member countries in the Third World, many of whom later became ministers of education. You also have the UNESCO Institute in Hamburg, with which I have been involved since it was established in the early 1950s. This institute played an important role in promoting exchanges of experiences between countries, as well as in starting ventures like IEA. We had meetings of directors of research institutes in the 1950s. And out of these meetings grew two things. One was the International Association for the Evaluation of Educational Achievement (IEA), and the other was the attempt to establish a new subdiscipline of education, comparative education. Those who founded the comparative education society for Europe first met in Hamburg, before holding a meeting in London in 1961. The first International Congress was held in Amsterdam in 1962. We had the most recent one in Athens in October 1996. So in that respect, UNESCO has been instrumental.

An international body the size of UNESCO, or other special agencies such as the WHO or FAO, is always at risk. Such agencies tend to become big and bureaucratized. They find it difficult to "simplify" themselves. At the beginning it was the opposite, all kinds of crazy ideas were accepted. That was during the Julian Huxley time as director general. I myself was involved in a project in Asia in 1967, when the UNESCO Education Department took the initiative to launch a workshop in Tokyo. Member countries in Asia were invited to send delegations with the purpose of identifying how one could develop research competence in education in Asian countries. The Japanese, who were rather advanced in this field, undertook the responsibility to follow up the workshop. We had two- or three-week workshops in Tokyo, which were then followed up by annual meetings under the auspices of the National Institute of Educational Research in Tokyo.

Why did the United States and the United Kingdom leave UNESCO?

I don't know. In a way there was a problem with them. The director general then, in my view, was a serious liability. I knew him fairly well. He became a member of the IIEP board in the early 1970s; and since I was the chairman of the board, I had quite a lot to do with him. The way he was running the show was not always very good for UNESCO. I hate to go into any details.

Is it fair to see his form of leadership as at least one reason for the United States and the United Kingdom leaving UNESCO?

This was one of the reasons. There also was the tendency of UNESCO to take a certain stand when it came to conflicts between the United States and the Soviet Union.

You touched on the IIEP. Could you briefly tell about how it came up and what your role was in establishing this institute?

As far as my role is concerned, it was rather modest and coincidental. In 1962 I was contacted by a Swedish colleague, a law professor. He had worked at the U.N. headquarters in New York, and then he became a member of the Swedish National Commission of UNESCO. He had been invited to become a member of a planning committee for an Institute of Education Planning. He may have been short of time so he asked me to serve instead of him. That is the way I came to be involved in drawing up a blueprint for a new institute with two main purposes. One was to train education planners in very concentrated one-year courses. I sometimes thought of these in terms of one-year master's courses. The second purpose was to do research: demography, curriculum, and general sociological studies, which were intended to provide a background for education planning in developing countries. The institute started in 1963, and Philip Coombs was its first director. I attended meetings during the 1960s. We had a very good meeting once on the quality of education in developing countries, and I think the report of that meeting, which came out in 1968 or 1969, is still relevant today. The institute came up with quite a lot of innovations, one was so-called mini-planning, or planning education at the local level. School mapping was another one.

Over the years quite a lot of research projects have been conducted. The IIEP consisted of a professional staff of some 15 people, a support staff of perhaps 20 to 25, and then some 40 trainees, or *stagières*, as they call them in French, who spent a year in Paris. They were young civil servants from developing countries. Several of them later became ministers of education.

Do you think IIEP is still adequate and relevant?

Since I have been retired for quite some time, I cannot pass judgment on IIEP's adequacy today. But to me it is obvious that the turnover of staff has been a bit too low. That applies to UNESCO as a whole. You should not be there for more than five or six years. I think there are staff members who have been there since 1970 when I took the chair at IIEP. That is 25 years ago. I visited IIEP recently, but just for a day, and talked with the director, Jacques Hallak, who by the way, joined the institute in the early 1960s. He was one of the first staff members that Philip Coombs hired.

Who was Philip Coombs?

Philip Coombs was the first director of IIEP. In the early 1960s he was a kind of assistant secretary of state dealing with cultural affairs in the U.S. Foreign Office. He was a kind of "vice minister" of education in the Kennedy Administration. His background was in economics, but during the war he worked in the Price Control Agency in Washington, D.C. He was the one who wrote the background document on the world crisis in education for the famous Williamsburg meeting in 1967.

How did you and Philip Coombs work together?

We worked very closely together, and we were both members of James Perkins' "mafia." Coombs was the vice chairman. James Perkins, the godfather, was the chairman. The organization's official name was International Council for Educational Development (ICED). It existed from 1970 until 1994.

What was the function and status of the International Bureau of Education in Geneva?

It was founded under the League of Nations in the early 1920s. In a way it was resuscitated after 1945. It later came under UNESCO.

William D. Halls has published a book about the state of the art of comparative education. IBE is the publishing agency. Do you know him?

Yes. I think IBE gave him the commission to do this. He was a member of my Academia Europea task force, which produced the report on *Schooling in Modern European Society* (1992).

Had he been attached to IBE?

He worked there for some time. IBE was instrumental in regularly getting together representatives from the ministries of education of the U.N. member countries. They held meetings centered on a particular problem area. There is a series of reports from these meetings. I assume IBE has now been dissolved and its tasks are to be taken over by the UNESCO Secretariat in Paris.

Some sort of structural rationalization?

Yes. I have followed this very closely. They also published the *Yearbook of Education.*

A final question about the United Nations and education. To your knowledge, besides UNESCO and UNICEF, are there other U.N. bodies that played a significant role in the field of education?

I don't know to what extent UNICEF has been important. But we had on the IIEP Board representatives of the World Health Organization as well as FAO, and I think they alternatively appointed a member to the board. The U.N. headquarters in New York had representatives for education. The IIEP had selected members and designated elected members. They were elected by the board. So the board renewed itself with certain members. The others were designated by various U.N. agencies.

Do you see any sort of contradiction between UNESCO and OECD in terms of their education policies?

I hate to rank them. The advantage for OECD is, of course, that it consists only of highly industrialized countries, which means that this is a much more homogeneous organization.

OECD has a particular purpose with its activities. It grew out of the Marshall Plan. Its overriding purpose is to promote economic growth. This is a very pragmatic goal, whereas the goals of UNESCO are much more diffuse. Since it has all the countries of the world as members, UNESCO has great difficulties in unifying the members around certain purposes. I used to illustrate the differences between the two by comparing the role of their secretariats. UNESCO is ruled by some 170 to 180 governments who try to have their say and try to push the Secretariat in one or another direction. In the case of OECD, as long as there were only 24 governments, the members were pushed by the Secretariat. The Secretariat of OECD wanted to move conservative governments. OECD tried to democratize education, taking advantage of the existence of the "talent reserve" of the populations. They had international seminars on this issue. They promoted OECD's policies through a strategy group of which I was a member for a certain time. They promoted studies that tried to identify future problems and challenges. They strongly promoted modernization of school curriculum.

Part Three
FUTURE

Global Education Trends at the Turn of the Century

We covered a great expanse of history, talking about Torsten Husén's work over more than five decades. Next, it was time to turn our thoughts to the future, to the new century and the new millennium.

I would like to move on to the future and ask you to speculate about the development of more privatized education.

If somebody had told me 20, or even 10 years ago, that we would have a growing private sector in education in Sweden, I would not have believed it. Private in the Swedish context means being rather independent of the government. But we now have a private sector, and something similar happened in the United States. The voucher system used to be very strongly rejected there because the common public school was supposed to be the backbone of the American democracy. They could with some hesitation accept the parochial schools, the Catholic schools. On the other hand, the voucher system is a choice given to the parents.

In a way, it depends on how you define private. The voucher system, both in the United States where it is in operation or in Sweden, means that money to run the school is given by the municipality or the state. It is public money, so in that respect it is a public school. Furthermore, schools must follow, at least in Sweden and I think the same is the case in the United States, the goals set for public schools. They cannot deviate strongly from the curriculum. In that respect there are limits to privatization.

Do you expect further privatization tendencies?

Yes. It will be necessary because of the difficulties in having steering mechanisms from some central place in the country, even in a region. I think there will be increased privatization, in the sense that the decisions affecting the daily affairs in the school will be taken at a local level, or even at the school-site level.

What do you foresee as future changes to curriculum internationally?

The universal tendency has been to broaden general education. It used to be common to see early differentiation as necessary. Not only educators, but also the general public and the politicians used to believe that once you had a few years of general education, say six years, then you had to begin to differentiate in various directions. When the 1946 Swedish School Commission submitted its main report in 1948, they thought there should be three tracks. First, the academic track, was for preparing for the upper secondary school, which in turn prepared for the university. Second, a vocational track, was for preparing for various types of vocations. There was further differentiation within this track. The third one was called the general track, which was some kind of mixture between the academic and the vocational track. Now we see a tendency based on the realization that the more basic general education you have, the more freedom you have in making choices later.

What do you think will happen to UNESCO in the next 50 or 100 years?

I think UNESCO has to rethink its role. According to its constitution UNESCO shall be an organization for promoting education, science, and culture, and in that role act as a peacemaker. They have to re-assess what to do in each of these fields. I cannot say anything about the fields of science and culture. Regarding education, I have been in touch with UNESCO since 1948, and I contributed to a chapter on education in the 50th-year *festschrift* of the organization.

I am convinced that one has to rethink the role in developing countries, along the lines that I have spelled out elsewhere, regarding the inadequacy of the Western model of formal education in the developing countries. I'm also convinced that one has to rethink the timetable for doing things. There has always been that kind of optimistic conception that you can change things, if not overnight, at least from one year to the other. In the first place, we have to see educational change in its socioeconomic context and to consider the role of education within the particular culture. Furthermore, we have to see changes in education in a wider time perspective.

How do you think the United States and the United Kingdom will relate to UNESCO in the future?

My guess is that it will not be very long until the United States and Britain are back again, not only as members, but also with their contributions. They cannot stay outside in the long run. I would guess that soon after the next presidential election, the United States will join again.

Because of a new ideology within UNESCO?

Not really. The reason why they left UNESCO, I gather, is that it was in the wake of the Cold War, but also dissatisfaction with the way the organization at that time was managed.

Has the leadership of UNESCO improved?

Yes. I think the new director general has done a good job in making the organization survive. When the two main contributors left, the situation was dramatic, since the United States alone contributed about one-quarter of the budget. They had to revise the whole organization to keep the programs going. As you can imagine, given the size of it, the cost of the Secretariat is enormous. I remember at the general conference in Nairobi in 1976, somebody asked how much of the UNESCO total budget was going to salaries for people sitting in Paris. I have forgotten the figure, but it was huge. It spotlighted the amount of resources used by the headquarters in Paris.

While UNESCO seems to have had a rather clear cultural-humanist perspective on the role of education in all countries, OECD has been preoccupied more with thinking about human capital and how education can be used as a creative force for business and the economy. Do you think these different roles will continue in the future?

The leading idea of UNESCO has been to promote peace, using as strategies education, science, and culture programs. OECD, as I said, grew out of the Marshall Plan and in its present form began in 1960. The overall purpose was, in the first place, to give Europe an economic boost. They were fortunate in that around 1960, leading economists in the field, among them Theodore Schultz in Chicago, Arthur Lewis in Princeton, Ingvar Svennilson in Stockholm, and Odd Aukrust in Oslo, began to look into this problem of how education is contributing to economic growth. Therefore OECD put a great deal of emphasis on education, particularly formal education but also on promotion of scientific research, particularly in technology and on applying science in technology.

What about CERI?

The Center for Educational Research and Innovation (CERI) was established in the late 1960s. It was conceived as a kind of semi-independent body within OECD. How independent it was is difficult to say, but it was a separate body in OECD. I cannot remember exactly when it was formed, but I would guess about 1968. It was established because there was a group of people in OECD at that time who were very optimistic about what education research would be able to do in terms of boosting economy. Thus they were very receptive to ideas from all kinds of directions. I remember it because I had quite a lot to do with OECD during these years. I even wrote a book on *Social Background and*

156

Educational Career that CERI commissioned. It came out in 1972, when I was a member of the so-called CERI Strategy Group. But they were also very interested in futuristic methods, and there was a group at Syracuse University working on these issues. I did a paper for OECD at that time, which was a kind of by-product of a project I was doing on Swedish education by the year 2000. So, OECD/CERI was seminal in promoting education as a means for economic growth, but also in promoting education research and innovative ideas in education that applied to the structure and the curriculum.

In addition to yourself, were other Scandinavians involved in OECD or UNESCO work?

From Scandinavia there were contributions by Kjell Eide from Norway, who had been employed at the Secretariat for some time and who was very active during the time when Ronald Gass was running CERI. Ingvar Svennilson, the economist at the University of Stockholm, was active. Per Dalin from Norway was on the OECD staff in the early 1970s. From these circles we got one of Kjell Härnqvist's doctoral candidates, Jarl Bengtsson. He came to OECD in 1971, and he is still there. The Swedish government, particularly the Ministry of Education, was very eager to have close contact with OECD.

Denmark joined the European Union in 1972, and Sweden and Finland in 1994. Norway preferred to stay out but is associated in important areas, education being one. What is your opinion about the EU's impact on education policy in the member countries?

Now EU is officially involved, according to the Maastricht Treaty. The previous treaties didn't have a single word about education. EEC grew out of the Steel and Coal Union, the Schumann Plan for European cooperation. I remember this because I was on the Continent in 1950 on behalf of the Swedish government, studying the psychological aspects of the propaganda in the Cold War, and at that time I met with a German professor in Bonn (I forget his name) who was one of the architects of the Schumann Plan. But there was not a single word in that long treaty about education. Neither was education mentioned in the Treaty of Rome. But in the Maastricht Treaty it is.

On behalf of the International Academy of Education, I once met with people who were dealing with education in the EU. The activities of the European Union are administrated in directorates. There was none in education, but one in human resources. And after all, human resources are created by education. Therefore they were interested in vocational education, not so much in school education. But I have heard now that they have become interested in education issues. So, I would guess it is just a matter of time before they have a general directorate for education as well. They have to discuss a budget for research, and part of it should go to education research.

Is it possible to foresee that the European Union will have something like a common curriculum?

Yes and no. I have been asked that question many times. Why not in Europe when they did it in the United States? But the United States was at the beginning a territory, where one in the first place had pushed the original inhabitants aside. It was dominated by Western culture, the white Anglo-Saxon Protestants, who were not governed from Washington, D.C. In the 1860s they established a bureau of statistics, which collected information about education. In the Constitution, education is not mentioned. In 1958 the National Defense Education Act passed under a false label to promote education in science and mathematics. But in the Constitution there were strict rules that nothing about religion, which is an important part of education, should be taught.

We cannot foresee any similar development in Europe because the curriculum in each country is so closely related to the respective national cultures, and with the national culture goes the history of the nation. In the United States there was no long history. They created history while building the school system. The EU can be doing what the Council of Europe did, going to the textbooks of history and trying to remove the kind of chauvinistic and biased description of European conflicts and things of that sort. Even though there is, as John Meyer and his people have shown in their studies of globalization of education, a kind of "approachment" among education systems, teaching still has to be conducted in the mother tongue, in the first place, and students need to be taught the history of the nation they belong to.

We must remember that when primary schools were established in Europe in the 19th century and became compulsory and universal in the respective countries, this was at the same time as the massive efforts to homogenize the countries. For instance, in France around 1870, only half the population in the area now called France spoke French. The same applied to other areas, such as Britain. In Wales they had their local language, but they had to learn English, as was the case in Ireland and in the north, where the Lapps had to learn Norwegian, or Swedish, or Finnish. So the very fact that you are taught in your mother tongue and that you are taught history and you are familiar with your particular national culture implies that we cannot foresee any common curriculum in Europe. But certain fields, like science and mathematics, are by nature international.

What about the future development of higher education? Will that be different?

Yes, this is different. And I have been very interested in studying historically the development of higher education in Europe and the tendency of students to go abroad. In the early days, Scandinavian students went to the continent. The leading universities, like Bologna, Salamanca, Leyden, and Paris, were located there. Paris is often identified as the oldest one, but Bologna is perhaps even older than Paris. In the 14th century came Oxford and Cambridge, and you had Prague and Krakow. Scandinavian students could get along in these universities because the teaching was done in Latin, which was for centuries the lingua franca in higher education, at least, at the leading universities. I have at home a Comenius textbook, called *The Doors of the Language*

Have Been Opened (*Janua Linguarum Reserata*), which came out in the first edition in 1632, 10 years before Comenius came to Sweden. On the inner cover of my book, a Swedish student by name Simon Segerdahl wrote: "Simon Segerdahl, legitime possesseur de ce livre. Paris" and a date, "April 1674." He was a student in Paris at that time, and he had a book with parallel texts in Latin and French. The book was published in several editions. They all had parallel languages. It could be Latin and French, or it could be Greek, as well, and German. This student had had Latin in school, of course. I could identify him because later on in the faculty at the University of Stockholm I had a colleague in statistics whose name was Segerdahl.

What we are seeing now is how English is becoming a lingua franca. The Erasmus program and all these other exchange programs going on will promote internationalization of higher education. I gather that there are several institutes here at the University in Oslo where they are beginning to use English as the medium of instruction.

Have you had study programs at the University of Stockholm using English as the language of instruction for quite a while?

Yes, since the 1960s. Gunnar Myrdal was the one who took the initiative in a master's program in the social sciences. It was called the Stockholm Graduate School for English-Speaking Students. Most of them, like Roland Paulston, who is American, came from English-speaking countries. But this was in the past. Now we have institutions where the medium of instruction is almost 100% English, in order to be able to serve students from developing countries. This applies to my institution, the one on international education at Stockholm University.

We have focused on Europe and the European Union. If you take a global perspective, can you see a movement to internationalize higher education further in Europe?

This is interesting, because in the 17th century Comenius had the idea to establish international centers where scholars could be

160

together. Comenius played an important role in promoting the idea of a center in Britain, which became a Royal Society. Frederic the Great of Prussia was interested in establishing something similar, an international center of scholars. So higher education had for a long time been quite "international," which meant European at that time. But then in the 18th and 19th centuries, the universities became more provincial, more national than they had been before. You can see this if you read the autobiography of Stanley Hall, an American. He looked at Europe with fresh eyes. He was a student in Germany in the 1870s and took his doctorate and even post-doctorate studies there. He later became president of Clark University and began his service as president by spending a year traveling around in Europe and describing his impressions. It is quite evident that at the end of the 19th century, the European universities were more provincial than they were 200 years earlier, during Comenius' time. Latin was used as the medium of instruction, and it did not matter whether you went to Oxford, Prague, or Salamanca, because they were to a large extent part of the same intellectual culture, not only through the language, but also because of the ecclesiastic elements in the scholarship they gave.

Thinking of higher education and internationalization today, and moving the perspective to developing countries, what is your feeling about what will happen to the research university in the developing countries?

I conducted a study on research competence in education in the developing countries for the World Bank. I concentrated on Asia, Africa, and Latin America. Later on, I went to Guadalajara in Mexico every year for a seminar on higher education where you got people from the major institutions in Latin America. What struck me then was the enormous provincialism, particularly in Latin America. I think that in Nairobi, university people were more internationally oriented than they were in Santiago, Rio, or Mexico City. I can give you one example. I gave lectures, in English, to the faculty in education, some 80 people at the University of Guadalajara. I noticed that a very high percentage of the audience needed to use simultaneous translation facilities. If you have a very limited understanding of English, you are severely handicapped in being part of the international community of scholars. I noticed in a country like Mexico that the leading intellectuals were part of a kind of Spanish culture and had much closer connections with Spain or even with the French-speaking part of the world.

Are you saying that it is an advantage to have been a British colony?

Yes, in a way it is. I think the British haven't been as aggressive as the French have been in promoting their own language. The French Ministry of Education contributed big sums to promote the French language in Francophone Africa. This was also a way of promoting French culture.

If we stay with the universities in developing countries, for instance in Africa, and you look ahead and take into account the paradox of the simultaneous mismatch and necessity of the Western model of schooling, do you think that African countries will be able to develop a particular African university model?

In commenting on this I have to be very cautious. The very idea of the university is that it is universal. It has three major roles. One is to extend the frontiers of knowledge, that is, to do research for its own sake. This can best be implemented in rich institutions and rich countries, which are not very dependent on a market. The second role, and most important one, is to train professionals, which was the original task of the university. They had to train priests, teachers, lawyers, medical doctors, and other professionals. And third, universities are to deliver services in a very wide sense, applying what there is in terms of basic knowledge to technology. The role of the modern university came up in the International Council for Education Development, where we dealt with it particularly in Third World countries.

In the Third World it will be particularly important for universities to offer their services to society. They cannot afford the aloofness possible in rich countries. So, my very simple idea is that, in a rich country's university you can afford to have people who are free. They can do research, whatever they want, without control or direction. My favorite example is the Finnish Academy. If you are a member there, you do exactly what you like. This is also true at the leading American universities where you have research professorships. The only limitation is the subject field in which you are supposed to do your work. But I do not think anybody is going to be hanged if he or she is doing things outside that field. So it is a matter of economy. It is, of course, very important to have people who are in such a situation because most of the breakthroughs in research have been done by people who were not aiming at a breakthrough. They just happened. Trial and error is in many respects a trademark of research.

To what degree do you think this Western ivory tower also could be a university model for Third World countries?

It is a matter of being able to afford it. The existence of think tanks can serve as an example. I don't know any Third World country that has been able to afford a think tank like the Princeton Institute for Advanced Study or its counterparts here in Europe (for example, the *Wissenschaftskolleg zu Berlin*). Some researchers are lifetime fellows, who do whatever they think is interesting. Of course, they have to qualify for it.

Aren't there contradictions here? Wouldn't a Westernization and elitist development of Third World universities create a serious tension with a primary and secondary education system that has to be locally oriented? Wouldn't the intellectual elite of the developing country become Westernized?

Westernization of the elite has already taken place, simply because a fairly high percentage of the elite in the developing countries have had their education at American and European universities. They are then a kind of role model. Their image of success is emulated at the lower levels of the system. And it is just a matter of time to arrange a kind of marriage between the national culture and the international university culture that they have been absorbing. This can sometimes be a very tough problem.

I observed a strange thing in an African country where the black elite in governmental positions and people of the university called each other comrade but as a rule sent their kids to private secondary boarding schools, which were completely staffed by teachers and a headmaster from England. How do you explain such behavior?

It is interesting. My first experience of Africa is from 1959, in a country where they were just in the process of getting independence. I had met the minister of planning, a very bright young man who had taken his academic degrees in Europe. I told him I would very much like to visit a school, and he brought me to a secondary school that was almost an ideal copy of a British public school. I listened to the lessons. All the teaching was done in English, and they studied British history. Latin and, I think, Greek were also on the curriculum. I gathered they had British textbooks. I said to the headmaster, "Don't you teach them African history and civics, studies about African society, and about problems you are encountering now when you are changing from colonial to independent status?" He looked as if I had insulted him and said, "Don't you think that we should have the same quality of schooling as our former colonial masters?" This gives a parallel to what you say about another African country. And it is like the experience I had in Britain about a decade later. There was a Royal Commission appointed by Anthony Crosland that had to take a look at the public schools: if and to what extent they should be supported and their future fate, so to speak. It was discovered then that several members of the elite of the Labour Party sent their sons to such schools.

Does this imply that the classic British liberal education institutions serve as role models not only for party members in England, but also for people in the former colonies?

164

Yes. What also struck me in Africa when I was involved in this planning exercise in Botswana, and also looking at the situation in the adjacent countries, was that they were using the Cambridge certificate as a kind of norm for their examinations.

Regarding higher education in developing countries, the World Bank has been criticized in relation to its aid policies in the field of education. What should the role of the World Bank be?

I am not very experienced, even though I was for sometime in close touch with people dealing with education in the World Bank, among them Mats Hultin, Duncan Ballantine, and Aklilu Habte. The World Bank is, like OECD, concerned with promoting economic "take off" in developing countries, which means that they have that kind of perspective on how they provide aid. On behalf of the World Bank I evaluated projects in three Latin American countries: El Salvador, Chile, and Colombia; and I also have been able to study its programs in Brazil. I know the controversy regarding the World Bank's role in education between the Marxist-oriented people on one hand and those more oriented towards the American mainstream on the other. But after all, the Americans have the strongest influence. I have been dealing with problems of what they refer to in the United States as the education gap, which I have written a bit about. I also wrote a memorandum for the World Bank on problems in secondary education common to the world today.

At the beginning, the World Bank did not deal with education. I think the first people in education came in the middle 1960s. I mentioned that I conducted a study on education research in Third World countries, particularly in Africa and Latin America. I was struck by the enormous gap in terms of resources, but also even more in terms of outcomes. Particularly in the Latin American countries productivity was dismal, though they have research institutions with sizable staff. In Africa I could identify four or five places where education research was conducted, leaving out South Africa, which was a white enterprise at that time. So, they have difficulties in getting research connected with teaching.

What do you think will happen to the IEA in the future?

That is indeed an important question for me. We meet once a year, to look at the kind of work that has been done, of course, in concrete projects, but also sometimes to discuss policy for the future. IEA is now in the midst of a project called TIMSS, Third International Science and Mathematics Study. At least 40 countries are participating. We were 12 at the beginning, all industrialized. We began by making comparisons in terms of competencies achieved in mathematics, science, and reading, and by explaining differences in terms of socioeconomic structure or background, in terms of school resources, and in terms of methods of teaching. These were the three sets of factors we wanted to study to account for the differences, both within and, particularly, between countries. What the policymakers as well as the media in most countries take interest in is the average level of competence achieved. There is very little interest in spread of achievements. There has been a tendency among international bodies like OECD to take advantage of the existence of the IEA. They want data for publications like *Education at a Glance* (1995), showing the standards achieved at regular intervals. It requires enormous resources to do these international surveys. It has become a multimillion dollar enterprise by now. When we did the first mathematics study in the 1960s, it was, all told, a one- or two-million dollar enterprise. Now it may be at least $100 million.

I would like for the IEA in the future to be a research organization primarily, not an organization running a kind of competitive Olympic intellectual games, which is very tempting. I guess there are many interesting things that IEA has not sufficiently elucidated. I am thinking of, for example, the differences between classrooms in Japan, Singapore, and China on the one hand, and classrooms in Zimbabwe, Botswana, Brazil, or the United States on the other. Some attempts have been made, for instance, by Harold Stevenson and his co-workers at the University of Michigan, but not on particularly representative groups. They have been looking into classrooms in Chicago, Taipei, Taiwan, Tokyo, and Beijing. They are trying to find out what is actually happening there. IEA has had very little observation and data to work with, which is also important to explain differences.

Which countries would you expect to be the most dynamic in the future in terms of education policies?

I hesitate to appoint any country to a kind of leadership. I think that countries with strong parental involvement at the local level will be more successful with their education systems. A general tendency seems to be that the parents are limiting their role more and more. I think this is one feature that I would like to emphasize. Another important feature is flexibility of organization in terms of differentiation. I think it is important that children are not put in tracks too early in their education career. Furthermore, establishing avenues of lifelong education for adults, lifelong in the sense of providing institutional opportunities, is important. I mean, adults can always find the opportunity of learning something new on their own, but there must also be institutions to help them do this. In that respect, I think the universities are going to play an important role. They can provide what is called in the United States "centers for continuing education."

Do you find it meaningful to talk about a Scandinavian, a Continental, a U.S., and an Asian model of formal education?

I think it is justified. The Continental school model is strongly what I would like to call a parallel model. Those who are considered academically promising are rather early separated from the rest, who are supposed to take vocational, manual, or nonmanual tracks, which require a specific type of training and knowledge. If you look at Germany, or even France, you still see this model, even though they are trying to provide opportunities for an increasing proportion of the age cohort to go on in school until they are 18. In France the target is that 60% will take the baccalaureate. This is not necessarily an academic baccalaureate; it could be a kind of diploma from vocational programs as well. The Scandinavian system has been successful in postponing this kind of differentiation as late as possible.

Torsten Husén works at a manual typewriter in his book-lined office at the University of Stockholm in 1995.

At home in March 1999, again surrounded by books, Husén poses for a picture in connection with an interview about his book, Insikter och Åsikter (Insights and Opinions), *which had just been published.*

In Europe, in general, schooling has been legislated for entire nations and governed from a central agency in the national capital. Parliament appropriates most of the money, at least for secondary education, and in Scandinavia, for half of the costs of primary schooling as well. In the United States the major portion of funding comes from either the community, the municipality, or the state. Legislation and funding have been more centralized in Europe than in the United States.

Comparing the quality of secondary school in Scandinavia and the United States, do you observe any particular differences?

The IEA studies show no more striking differences between Scandinavia and the United States in mass secondary education. We have the same problem as the Americans, perhaps not as serious as they had, in recruiting good teachers who are competent in such fields as science, for instance. The recruitment of science and mathematics teachers has been a disastrous area in the United States. But we are getting that problem in Europe now as well.

Which countries, then, do you think have the best teachers in mathematics and science?

I think Japan. The profession is still attractive. They are relatively well paid, relatively well respected, they are looked up to by the rest of the society, and a teacher has authority, which he or she no longer has in Europe and the United States.

What do you think will be the future role of comparative education research in terms of projects similar to the IEA studies?

The IEA has, so far, been limited to empirical studies. Before IEA launched mathematics studies in the 1960s, comparative education research looked at the development of systems by describing the structure and curricula based on existing documents. IEA introduced strict empirical methods and internationally valid measurements, using standardized questionnaires. All the instruments were standardized because they were used cross-nationally. A further

169

challenge for IEA is to conduct observational studies in a systematic way.

Finally, Torsten Husén, what would be your dream research project?

It would be a comparative study of education reforms, and the extent to which what I call the "strategic principles" have been followed. I have recently spelled out these principles in various contexts, trying to answer the question to what extent they apply to education change occurring within the framework of change in socioeconomic context. How much time does it take to prepare, draw up the blueprint, get it through the political process, and implement it in the classrooms. Further, it is of great interest to get more insights about the role of participation of those who are affected, parents, local politicians, and so forth. Then there is the cost connected with these processes. The historical aspect of the changes over time is also of interest. This, I think, would be a big, important, and challenging project.

If you look at what has happened in Europe since 1945, you find there are fantastic changes in all respects, taking place everywhere in Europe, not least in Scandinavia. There are also changes taking place, of course, in certain developing countries. But they are in many respects taking over models from the West, and then the issue of relevancy must arise. The question of relevant education in rich and industrialized countries is how to organize it so that people can learn for the rest of their lives, whereas in the developing countries the problem is to at least see to it that they have some primary education and not put all the resources into secondary and higher education.

I think such a project would be of interest because it could teach us quite a lot, particularly to provide ammunition against those who think you can change an education system overnight.

Acronyms and Abbreviations

Throughout this work a number of organizations are referred to by their abbreviation or acronym. This list may be helpful.

ABF	The Workers' Study Organization in Sweden
AERA	American Educational Research Association
CERI	Center of Educational Research and Innovation
CESE	Comparative Education Society for Europe
ETS	Educational Testing Service (Princeton, New Jersey)
EU	European Union
FAO	Food and Agriculture Organization (United Nations)
IBE	International Bureau of Education
ICED	International Council for Educational Development
IEA	International Association for the Evaluation of Educational Achievement
IIEP	International Institute for Educational Planning
LO	Central Federation of Trade Unions (Sweden)
NATO	North Atlantic Treaty Organization
OECD	Organisation for Economic Co-operation and Development
SACO	Federation of Swedish Academics
UNDP	United Nations Development Program
UNESCO	United Nations Educational, Scientific and Cultural Organization
UNICEF	United Nations Children's Fund
WB	The World Bank
WHO	World Health Organization

Brief Biography of Torsten Husén

Although the conversations and interviews compiled in this work convey a sense of Husén's life and works, the following succinct biography is intended to provide a general, cohesive overview.

Academic Career. Torsten Husén graduated in 1937 from the University of Lund, where he also took his Ph.D. in 1944. He worked at his alma mater as an instructor and research assistant between 1938 and 1944. During World War II (1942-44) he was an Army staff psychologist. He worked as a senior psychologist at the Swedish Central Bureau of Conscription until 1952, and was at the same time an associate professor at Stockholm University. From 1953 to 1956 he was professor and chair of Educational Psychology at Stockholm University. From 1956 until 1971 he was director of the Institute of Educational Research at the School of Education, Stockholm. He established the Institute of International Education at Stockholm University in 1971 and was its director until 1982, when he formally retired as professor emeritus.

Institutional Governance. Husén was chairman of the governing board of the Extramural Department, Stockholm University (1953-73); chairman of the governing board of the Folk University of Sweden (1955-73); chairman of the International Association for the Evaluation of Educational Achievement (IEA) (1962-78) and honorary president of the IEA since 1978; chairman of the governing board of the International Institute for Educational Planning (IIEP) in Paris (1970-80); trustee of the International Council for Educational Development (1971-93); and president of the International Academy of Education (1986-98).

Commissions. Torsten Husén has been an expert member of several Swedish and international commissions, among them: member of the Swedish Royal Commission on Juvenile Delinquency (1956-65), the Swedish Royal Commission on Teacher

Education (1962-65), the Government Panel of Scientific Advisors (1962-69), and the Council of Psychological Defense (1954-70). He has been a consultant to OECD, the World Bank, the U.N. University, and the Club of Rome and has been a member of various UNESCO task forces. He was the chairman of the National Commission on Education in Botswana (1976-77) and the chairman of the Academia Europaea Task Force on Basic Education in an Integrated Europe (1988-91).

Fellowships and Visiting Professorships. He has been a fellow at the Center for Advanced Study in the Behavioural Sciences, Stanford University (1965-66 and 1973-74); the National Humanities Center, University of North Carolina (1978-79); and the Institute for Advanced Study, Berlin (1984). He was a visiting professor at the University of Chicago (1959), the University of Hawaii (1968), Ontario Institute for Studies in Education (1971), Stanford University (1981), University of California at Berkeley (1984), and the Hoover Institution at Stanford (1993).

Editorial Boards. Husén served on the advisory editorial board of the *International Encyclopedia of Higher Education* (1972-76) and has been co-editor-in-chief of the *International Encyclopedia of Education* since 1981. He has been a member of the editorial board of several journals, including the *Teachers College Record*, *Comparative Education Review*, and the *International Journal of Educational Research*. He has been a contributor to the *Swedish National Encyclopedia*.

Academy Memberships. Torsten Husén is a member of the U.S. National Academy of Education (since 1967), the Royal Swedish Academy of Sciences (1972), the Finnish Academy (1974), the Polish Academy (1977), the American Academy of Arts and Sciences (1982), Academia Europaea (1988), and the Russian Academy of Pedagogical Sciences (1991).

Awards. Husén was awarded a Colombia University Teachers College Medal for Distinguished Service (1970). He has been awarded honorary doctorates at the following institutions: University of Chicago (1967), University of Glasgow (1974), Brunel University (1974), University of Rhode Island (1975), University of Joensuu (1979), University of Amsterdam (1982), and Ohio State University (1985). He was awarded the (Japanese) National Institute of Educational Research's Gold Medal (1983), an honorary professorship at the University of Shanghai (1984), the Cultural Prize of the *Natur & Kultur* Publishing House (1979), and the Comenius Medal (1994).

Selected Publications

1944. *Svensk Ungdom.* (Adolescence). Stockholm: Gebers.

1948. *Begåvning och Miljö.* (Ability and Milieu). Stockholm: Almqvist and Wiksell.

1950. *Testresultatens Prognosvärde.* (The Predictive Value of Test Scores). Stockholm: Almqvist and Wiksell.

1953. *Tvillingstudier.* (Psychological Twin Studies). Stockholm: Almqvist and Wiksell.

1967. (editor) *International Study of Achievement in Mathematics: A Comparison of Twelve Countries.* Stockholm: Almqvist and Wiksell; New York: John Wiley. 2 vols.

1969. *Talent, Opportunity, and Career.* Stockholm: Almqvist and Wiksell.

1971. *Utbildning År 2000.* (Education in the Year 2000). Stockholm: Bonniers. Published in six languages.

1974. *The Learning Society.* London: Methuen.

1974. *Talent, Equality, and Meritocracy.* The Hague: Martinus Nijhoff.

1975. *Influence du Milieu Social sur la Réussite Scolaire.* (Social Influences on Educational Attainment). Paris: CERI/OECD.

1977. *Jämlikhet Genom Utbildning?* (Education for Equality?). Stockholm: Natur och Kultur.

1979. *The School in Question: A Comparative Study of the School and Its Future in Western Societies.* Oxford: Pergamon Press. Published in 10 languages.

1983. *An Incurable Academic: Memoirs of a Professor.* Oxford: Pergamon Press.

1986. *The Learning Society Revisited.* Oxford: Pergamon Press.

1990. *Education and the Global Concern.* Oxford: Pergamon Press.

1992. *Möten med Psykologer, Pedagoger och Andra.* (Encounters with Psychologists, Educators and Others). Wiken: Höganäs.

1959. (editor, with S. Henrysson). *Differentiation and Guidance in the Comprehensive School.* Stockholm: Almqvist & Wiksell.

1967. (with G. Boal) *Educational Research and Educational Change: The Case of Sweden.* Stockholm: Almqvist and Wiksell; New York: John Wiley.

1984. (editor, with M. Kogan). *Educational Research and Policy: How Do They Relate?* Oxford: Pergamon Press.

1985. (with J.S. Coleman) *Becoming Adult in a Changing Society.* Paris: OECD.

1985. (editor, with T.N. Postlethwaite). *The International Encyclopedia of Education.* Oxford: Pergamon Press. 10 vols. 2nd ed. 1994.

1991. (editor, with J.P. Keeves) *Issues in Science Education: Science Competence in a Social and Ecological Context.* Oxford: Pergamon Press.

1992. (editor, with A. Tuijnman and W.D. Halls). *Schooling in Modern European Society: A Report of the Academia Europaea.* Oxford: Pergamon Press.

Bibliography

Adorno, T.W.; Frenkel-Brunswik, E.; Levinson, D.J.; and Sanford, R. Nevitt. *The Authoritarian Personality*. New York: Harper and Brothers, 1950.

Becker, Gary. *Human Capital*. New York: Columbia University Press, 1964.

Bloom, Benjamin. *Individual Differences: A Vanishing Point in School Achievement*. Bloomington, Ind.: Phi Delta Kappa, 1971.

Bühler, Karl. *Sprachtheorie*. Jena: Springer, 1934.

Coleman, James S., and Hoffer, T.B. *Public and Private High Schools*. New York: Basic Books, 1987.

Coleman, J.S., and Husén, T. *Becoming Adult in a Changing Society*. Paris: OECD, 1985.

Comenius, J.A. *Jenua Linguarum Reserata*. (The Doors of the Language Have Been Opened). Amsterdam: Elzevir, 1632.

Corey, Stephen. *Action Research*. New York: Columbia University, 1954.

Cremin, Lawrence. *American Education*. 3 vols. New York: Harper & Row, 1972-1988.

Delors, Jacques, et al. *Learning: The Treasure Within. Report of the International Commission on Education for the Twenty-First Century*. Paris: UNESCO, 1996.

Grimberg, Carl. *Svenska Folkets Underbara Oeden*. (The Wonderful Destiny of the Swedish People), 9 vols. Stockhom: Norstedt, 1914.

Hallgren, Siver. *Grupptestning*. (Group Testing). Stockholm: Almqvist and Wiksell, 1943.

Husén, T. *Testresultatens Prognosevärde*. (The Predictive Value of Test Scores). Stockholm: Almqvist and Wiksell, 1950.

Husén, T. "The Influence of Schooling Upon IQ." *Theoria* 17 (1951): 61-88.

Husén, T. "Resa i Amerikansk Pedagogik." (A Journey in American Education). In *Pedagogisk Debatti* 3, no. 2 (1955): 39-48; no 4 (1955): 114-21.

Husén, T. *Pedagogisk Psykologi*. (Educational Psychology). Stockholm: Svenska Bokförlaget, 1957.

Husén, T. *Vuxna Lär*. (Adult Learning). Stockholm: Ehlins, T.H., 1958.

Husén, T. *Skolan I ett Foranderligt Samhalle*. (The School in a Changing Society). Stockholm: Almqvist and Wiksell, 1961.

Husén, T. *Differensieringsproblem i Svensk Obligatorisk Skola*. (Problems of Differentiation in Swedish Compulsory Schooling). Stockholm: Svenska Bokförlaget (Norstedt), 1962.

Husén, T. "Vuxenpedagogiska Seminariet 10 År." (The Adult Education Seminar in Ten Years). *Folkuniversitetet* 15, no. 4 (1963): 15-21.

Husén, T. *Vad Lararutbildningen Galler: Ett Dedattinlägg*. (What Teacher Training Is About). Stockholm: Almqvist and Wiksell, 1966.

Husén, T., ed. *International Study of Achievement in Mathematics: A Comparison of Twelve Countries*. 2 vols. Stockholm: Almqvist and Wiksell; New York: John Wiley, 1967.

Husén, T. *Talent, Opportunity, and Career*. Stockholm: Almqvist and Wiksell, 1969.

Husén, T. *Skolans Kris*. (The School's Crisis). Stockholm: Almqvist and Wiksell, 1972.

Husén, T. *Social Background and Educational Career*. Paris: OECD, 1972.

Husén, T. *Universiteten och Forskningen*. (Universities and Research). Stockholm: Natur och Kultur, 1975.

Husén, T. *Jämlikhet Genom Utbildning?* (Equality by Education?). Stockholm: Natur och Kultur, 1977.

Husén, T. *The School in Question: A Comparative Study of the School and Its Future in Western Societies*. London: Oxford University Press; New York: Pergamon Press, 1979.

Husén, T. *An Incurable Academic: Memoirs of a Professor*. New York: Pergamon Press, 1983.

Husén, T. *Vad Har Hänt med Skolan? Perspektiv på Skolareformarna*. (What Has Happened to the School? Perspectives on the School Reforms). Stockholm: Verbum Gothia, 1987.

Husén, T. "Educational Research at the Crossroads." *Prospects* 19, no. 3 (1989): 351-60.

Husén, T. *Möten med Psykologer, Pedagoger och Andra*. (Encounters with Psychologists, Educators and Others). Wiken: Höganäs, 1992.

Husén, T. "Making School Reforms by Slogan." *The European*, 25 October 1995.

Husén, T. "Pedagogiken: En Vetenskap?" (Education: A Science?). *Svenska Dagbladet*, 3 March 1996.

Husén, T. *Insikter och Åsikter om Utbildningssämhället.* (Insights and Opinions About the Learning Society). Stockholm: Gothia, 1999.

Husén, T., et al. *The Six Subject Survey.* Prefaces to 9 vols. Stockholm: Almqvist and Wiksell; New York: John Wiley, 1973-1976.

Husén, T., et al. *Europaskolan.* Stockholm: Fritzes, 1995.

Husén, T., and Kogan, M., eds. *Educational Research and Policy: How Do They Relate?* Oxford: Pergamon Press, 1984.

Husén, T., and Postlethwaithe, T.N., eds. *The International Encyclopedia of Education.* 10 vols. Oxford: Pergamon Press, 1985. 2nd ed. 1994.

Husén, T.; Tuijnanman, A.; and Halls, W.D., eds. *Schooling in Modern European Society: A Report of the Academia Europaea.* Oxford: Pergamon Press, 1992.

Hutchins, Robert M. *Higher Learning in America.* New Haven, Conn.: Yale University Press, 1936.

Illich, Ivan. *Deschooling Society.* New York: Harper & Row, 1971.

James, William. *Talks to Teachers on Psychology.* London: Longmans, Green, and Co., 1899.

Kerr, Clark. *The Uses of the University.* Cambridge, Mass.: Harvard University Press, 1963.

Kelly, Allison. *Girls and Science.* Stockholm: Stockholm University Press, 1978.

Landquist, J. *Viljan.* (The Will). Stockholm: Bonniers, 1908.

Myrdal, Gunnar. *An American Dilemma.* 2 vols. New York: Harper & Row, 1944.

Myrdal, Gunnar, and Myrdal, Alva. *Kontakt med Amerika.* (Contact with America). Stockholm: Bonniers, 1943.

Organisation for Economic Co-operation and Development. *Education at a Glance: OECD Indicators.* Paris, 1995.

Picht, Georg. *Die Deutsche Bildungskatastrophe.* (The German Education Catastrophe). Olten, Freiburg: Walter, 1964.

Riis, Ulla, and Lindberg, Leif. *Värdering av Kvinnors Respektive Mäns Meriter vid Tjänstetillsaetning Inom Universitet och Högskolor.* (Evaluation of Merits of Men and Women in Connection with Promotion at Swedish Universities and Other Institutions of Higher Learning). Stockholm: Ministry of Education, 1996.

Skinner, B.F., and Vaughan, M.E. *Enjoy Old Age.* New York: W.W. Norton, 1983.

UNESCO. *Fifty Years for Education.* Paris, 1996.

Young, Michael. *The Rise of the Meritocracy*. London: Thames and Hudson, 1958.

Zhao, Shangwu. *Chinese Science Education: A Comparative Study*. Stockholm: Stockholm University Institute of International Education, 1993.

About the Author

Arild Tjeldvoll is a professor of comparative education at the University of Oslo. His research interests include education policy, professionalization of teaching, school management, higher education policies, human rights education, and development aid. He has traveled extensively and was visiting professor in Brazil, Estonia, several universities in the United States, South Africa, Sweden, and Zimbabwe. Under the sponsorship of several Norwegian government ministries, he worked with the Council of Europe, UNICEF, the European Union, Amnesty International, and other entities. He is chairman of the Committee for International Affairs in the Faculty of Social Sciences at the University of Oslo and a member of the Norwegian Research Council, Human Rights Association. Tjeldvoll is on the editorial board of *European Education*. He also was the initiator of the Nordic Network of International and Comparative Education (NICE). Tjeldvoll holds an advanced degree in sociology of education and his Ph.D. is from the University of Oslo.

About the Editor

Hans G. Lingens teaches in the School of Education at California Lutheran University. He joined the university after 25 years as teacher and researcher in the Los Angeles Unified School District. A native of Germany, Lingens studied natural sciences at the University of Cologne and received his M.A. and Ed.D. from the University of Southern California in curriculum and instruction and international education. His research interests include teacher education, higher education policy development, and comparative and international education. His travel and studies of other education systems have taken him to China, South Africa, the Americas, and Europe. He is editor of *European Education*.